Forty Days
Across America

ANDY HILL

ISBN-13: 978-1983733352
ISBN-10: 1983733350

DEDICATION

To Helen

CONTENTS

ACKNOWLEDGMENTS

Thanks to Tim Ralph, my partner in this adventure, without whose company and unwavering support I could not have done the ride. You can find Tim's mountaineering and cycling blog at: www.timralph.co.uk

The front and rear cover main photos were taken by a family who we met on the pass

The rear cover bison photo was taken by Tim Ralph

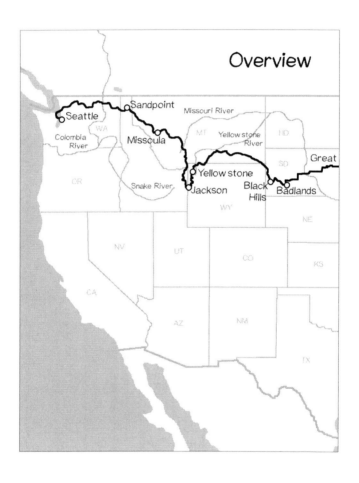

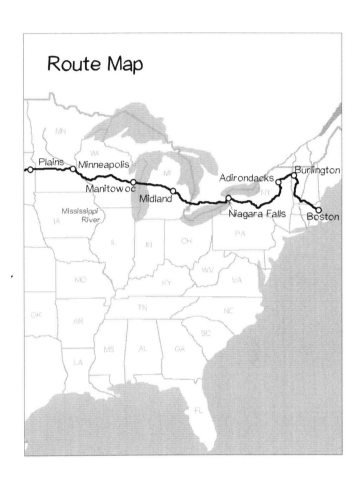

Route Map

1 PUGET SOUND AND THE SKAGIT RIVER

"Hey, are you guys really doing that, right now?"

Tim and I would get used to this question, usually delivered in a tone that we fondly imagined was astonished awe. The enquiry may have had something to do with the fact that we wearing cycling jerseys that proclaimed, 'Seattle to Boston – 4000 miles – 40 days' in letters several inches high across our chests, and there was a map to prove it. I couldn't help the huge grin that spread across my face as I replied,

"Yes, we really are doing it. Right here, right now."

We were standing on the deck of a car ferry, pulling away from the waterfront at Seattle, heading out across the Puget Sound. But this fellow passenger did not seem impressed. She seemed puzzled – perhaps even concerned.

"Well you do know that we're heading out west for Bainbridge Island, don't you ….?"

The silence that followed was awkward, as she and I lent on the rail and watched the skyline of Seattle receding in the ferry's sun-dazzled wake. The slogans on our shirts seemed to imply that we intended to travel east from

Seattle, by bicycle, and yet here we were, heading by boat in entirely the opposite direction. As potential transcontinental cyclists, I could see that our navigational competence was in some considerable doubt, and we hadn't even started cycling yet.

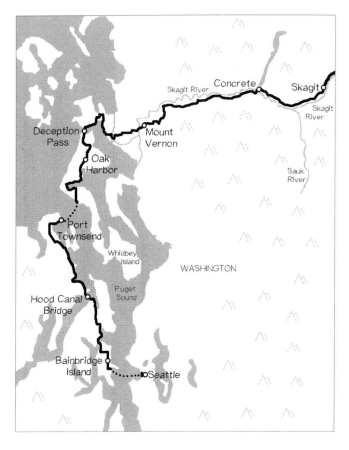

I duly explained to the relieved, but still puzzled enquirer, that we did indeed intend to go first to Bainbridge Island - and the contorted geography of our route plan thereafter. I didn't even attempt to explain the even more contorted psychology. The truth is that setting off to cycle across America seemed an almost impossibly daunting task. So, what could be better than starting out in the wrong direction and adding a bit more? It's as silly as the whole ride itself, and it's a psychological two fingers up to adversity. What's an extra few miles in the face of a whole continent? More important, we were determined to seek out the most spectacular sights and scenery along the way. Instead of the obvious route, via the traffic-laden eastern suburbs of Seattle and the Interstate 90 over the Stevens Pass, we were heading westwards, to seek out the delights of empty coast roads and stunning views across the Puget Sound, a two-mile-long floating bridge, another ferry, and some high and very remote passes over the northern Cascades. I am not sure whether to describe this as the romantic route, or the stupid route. It was certainly our route, and we were committed to it. So long as the cycling's good, who cares if, after our first day, we were destined to end up even further from Boston than when we started?

Such was the state of care-free euphoria with which the ride began, after more than two years of planning and anticipation. Seattle was enjoying a heat wave and, after what passes for early summer at home in the UK, so were we. In fact, the whole of the USA was in holiday mood because this was July 4th, Independence Day. Checking out of our hotel early that morning we had had the streets of Seattle to ourselves as we rolled down a couple of blocks to the sea at Waterfront Park, our 'official' starting point. We had intended to bookend our coast-to-coast cycle ride with two well-photographed wheel-dipping ceremonies: rear wheel in the sea at the start (nervously), and front wheel at the opposite coast (triumphantly). But when we arrived, it became clear that wheel-dipping at Waterfront Park was going to be impossible. The park is built on wooden piers, jutting out over the water. The sea was about 20 feet below the railing and there was no ladder access. The only other people around were sleeping rough, and they were huddled up in cardboard and old sleeping bags, completely out of it. We finally talked a rather taciturn dog-walker into taking our departure photograph by the rail, before rolling the very short distance down the road to the ferry terminal.

I have always enjoyed punctuating my bike rides with ferry crossings. Being on board a ferry as it glides smoothly and effortlessly across calm water reminds me of cycling, albeit on smooth tarmac with a tailwind. My favourite kind of cycling. And it's usually a relief to stop pedalling for a bit, although that hardly applied here, given that we had only clocked just over a mile so far. This time it was the scenery, and the anticipation of what lay ahead, that made the crossing so memorable. In one direction was the skyline of Seattle, with the symmetrical, volcanic dome of Mount Rainier apparently floating above it. Rainier's snow-capped peak was dazzling white against the bright blue sky. It didn't look real, more like a cartoon representation of a volcano. In the other direction, westwards over the top of Bainbridge Island, lay the jagged peaks of the Olympic Mountains, some still with snow on top. And whichever way you looked, the sparkling waters of the Puget Sound led to heavily forested shorelines and tiny islands, often above small, granite crags. Although I was keen to start cycling, another part of me just wanted these views, and this sense of contented, suspended animation, to go on forever.

It didn't. Leaving the ferry, we were straight into the well-heeled commuter township of Wilmslow. Here we were delighted to find that everything had been organised to give us a grand send off. The streets were closed to traffic for our passage; there were crowds of people and bunting everywhere, and rows of spectator chairs alongside the road. Then we remembered it was July 4th. Nonetheless, we waved royally to some very keen spectators who had bagged the best seats early, ahead of the carnival parade, but we received only mystified looks in return. Oh well. At least we didn't run anyone over as we weaved our way carefully through between the families wandering about the road, with heads down and hands full of pizza, burgers, and cartons of cola.

It was quite a wrench to ride away from the relaxed atmosphere of sedentary fun, food, and frivolity in town, but we were destined for a very different aesthetic. As though to rub it in, the road reared up immediately as we tackled our first climb, steeply up through natural pine woods on a minor road with no other sign of humanity. Not for us the burgers, chips, and dancing girls. Ours was to be the austere world of endurance cycling - blood, sweat and tears on remote country roads. Forty days is, after all, the appropriate length of time for being tested in the wilderness, though I should make it clear that neither of us is the Messiah. More like two very naughty boys.

At the northern end of Bainbridge Island, we came to the Agate Pass. This was the first pass that I had ever crossed that did not involve any ascent or descent at all. The Agate Pass is at sea level. It's a narrow tidal passage between Bainbridge Island and the mainland of the Kitsap Peninsula, the home of the Squamish people. There is now a road bridge across the strait, where we stopped for photos. If only all passes were all like this, then all that stupid cycling uphill would be redundant. When the Vancouver expedition of 1792 first mapped the area, they missed the Agate Pass altogether and for years it was assumed that Bainbridge Island was connected to the mainland. It took until 1841 to correct the mistake, until 1950 for the bridge to be built, and until this century for senior Amazon executives to build their luxury homes in township of Squamish, now a short commute by car and ferry from Amazon's vast new downtown campus in Seattle.

Before setting off we had spent a couple of enjoyable days looking around Seattle. Apart from Amazon and Starbucks, Seattle is also known as the home of Boeing, and we had a great time wandering around the Museum of Flight. The Museum is right next to Boeing Headquarters on Boeing Field – still in use as an airport today. In addition to the impressive array of aircraft, we visited the original wooden buildings where the earliest planes were built. Quite the best air museum I have ever seen.

But not everyone in Seattle is engaged in aviation or high-tech industry. As we wandered the streets, the obvious scale of homelessness and mental distress was quite shocking. Our ride on the crowded number 124 bus out to Boeing Field, for example, featured a memorable cast list of characters. Tim listed them on his blog. There was a woman completely absorbed in an endless, and very loud, monologue directed at her aging Golden Labrador. There was an elderly man meticulously rolling, and then unrolling a cigarette, over and over again. There was a young man who spent the journey eyeballing others, and who then pulled the 'stop' cord nearly off the wall, before rushing through the bus shouting at people as he jumped off. There was a middle-aged woman pouring out her intimate life story to an embarrassed-looking stranger squashed in the next seat. There was a young black man wearing a duffle coat over a down jacket and a woolly hat, when the temperature outside was around 90F and inside it was hot enough to melt steel. But then, we were about to spend six weeks in tight fitting lycra, pedalling across the USA, so who am I to point the finger?

Anyway, we had problems of our own. Once we had recovered from the onerous crossing of the vertiginous Agate Pass, Tim had a rear wheel puncture. As I waited for him to fix it, I couldn't help doing the maths. Fortunately, with almost exactly ten miles travelled, this was easy. At this rate, I announced, we could look forward to 400 punctures between here and Boston. This was worrying, since we had only one spare tube and a few patches each. We tried not to feel deflated.

One striking feature of the coastal villages hereabouts is

that they look just like the historic townships of New England. Arriving in Port Gamble, our first planned stop, I had a momentary feeling that I must have slept through a few thousand miles and that we were already in one of the villages outside Boston. The beautifully kept houses were wooden, with painted clapboard, usually white. They had steeply pitched roofs, and ornate verandas, sporting the Star-Spangled Banner all year round and not just on July 4th. Lawns were beautifully manicured, and there were no fences separating the properties. Port Gamble was a gem. The explanation for the architectural similarity with New England is straightforward. In the 1860s, when William Talbot was looking for labour to operate the sawmill he had just opened in Port Gamble, he recruited experienced workers and brought them West from the sawmills of Maine. The houses they built reflected the architecture of home.

We enjoyed our first coffee and cake of the trip in the garden of the very posh general store cum café, with a stunning view out over the Puget Sound. Straight away, our shirts and bikes attracted much attention.

"You guys have a support vehicle, though, hey?" was another question that we'd get used to in the coming weeks. This time it was our lightweight, carbon-fibre, Bianchi road bikes and minimal luggage that was causing the stir. We each had a small dry bag, slung under the back of the saddle, and a thin bag under the cross bar.

"No, no. You are looking at the entire expedition. We're travelling light".

And indeed, we were, with basically just a change of clothes for the evening.

It might have been possible to talk some poor sod into the tedium of low-speed driving across the USA in support of us, but I really didn't want to do so. Ok, I admit it. Our respective wives were in the frame for about a microsecond - in other words, until they got wind of the idea. But having done a lot of very happy long-distance touring cycling over the years with my wife, Helen, I was used to independent travel. I didn't want to be tied to a car, and Helen certainly didn't want to be driving it. I also knew it would undermine my mental resolve. As soon as the going got tough I would be wasting a lot of mental energy fighting the urge to get in the vehicle, and I didn't want that. Far better to have no back up plan, and no alternative but to keep pedalling! The only concession was that we had reserved accommodation for every night all the way across the USA. And by the wonders of internet booking, we even had free cancellation most nights, in case of emergencies.

Much of the riding so far that first morning had been through wooded country, with only occasional glimpses of the sea. So, after Port Gamble, it was great to be back on the open water, in the middle of the Puget Sound, with views all round, and the Olympic Mountains ahead. Only this time there was no ferry. We were crossing the Hood Canal Bridge, though the name is very misleading. First, the Hood Canal is not a man-made canal – it is a natural arm of the Puget Sound, a salt-water, tidal estuary with a big tidal range and fast currents. The Hood Canal separates the Kitsap Peninsula from the Olympic Peninsula. Second, the Bridge is mostly not a bridge – it is a series of floating pontoons with a roadway on top. It has a retractable central section to allow big boats through, and a short and low bridge section at the eastern end for small boats. The big boats in question are Trident submarines going to and from the nuclear weapons store at Bangor, though I probably shouldn't have told you that. The most impressive thing about the bridge is its length. The floating section is 1.25 miles long. For the cyclist, this section offers not only great views, but also the only flat ground that we encountered all day. The drawback was that short sections of concrete roadway were interspersed with steel grating, through which you could see the sea below. This grating was both slippery and rough, and we had read scary reports that suggested that the bridge was a sort of cycling skittle alley. We took it easy, with regular stops for photos, and came across unscathed.

Shortly before Port Townsend we joined Highway 20. This was a significant moment, first because the junction marked the most westerly point of our ride. From here on we'd be travelling in the correct direction – or so we hoped. Second, this was the road that we'd be following east for the next four days or so. First impressions were favourable, as it carried us quickly downhill into Port Townsend for lunch. This Victorian seaport promotes itself as 'the home of artists, musicians, dreamers, thinkers, and visionaries', so you get the picture. It has Writers' Workshops, a Kinetic Sculpture Race, and an International Film Festival. It also has some lovely old buildings, one of which housed a hippy style café. By this time, it was seriously hot, so we were happy to sit indoors in the cool. And here started a tradition that lasted for the remainder of the trip. Chicken salad and vast quantities of (non-alcoholic) liquid for lunch. Protein rich, but not stodgy, these chicken salads were perfect hot weather, mid-ride meals, and by the end we had sampled many different styles and counted ourselves connoisseurs. Our Guide to the Chicken Salads of the Northern USA will soon be available at all good bookshops.

Our second ferry trip of the day took us back east across the Puget Sound to Whidbey Island. In planning the overall route, I had been slightly concerned that, by leaving from Seattle, we would not be starting from the Pacific Coast itself, but some distance inland. Can you really claim to have cycled from the Pacific to the Atlantic if you never actually saw the former? This ferry ride was designed to give us a clear view out down the Strait of Juan de Fuca to the open Pacific, and it didn't disappoint. We passed close to a huge container ship that was heading out to sea from Seattle and, as we watched, it shrank slowly towards the distant, uninterrupted blue horizon between the Olympic

Peninsula to the south and Vancouver Island to the north. The Pacific Ocean!

"Wow. A thousand miles a day. You guys must be fit".

The shirts were getting us noticed again, this time by a young couple with two school aged children, obviously on holiday. But I wasn't quite sure how to correct Dad's mental arithmetic, whilst acknowledging the friendliness of the compliment. I didn't want to give offence.

"Mmmm..." I ventured. "We were hoping it'll be more like a hundred miles a day".

The kids giggled, but their Dad looked daggers at me. He was clearly not amused.

"Anyway", I hurried on, "it's a lot of cycling, and we're looking forward to seeing your beautiful country. Where are you from?"

Luckily, Mum picked up her cue and rescued me by talking about the attractions of their home town of Tucson, down south in Arizona, quite close to the Mexican border. Unfortunately, having studied the huge map on the front of my jersey, with our route laid out clearly across all the northern states, her next question was

"Are you going through Arizona?" The kids giggled again, and this time so did I.

On Whidbey Island, we spent a happy afternoon pedalling the coast road to our motel, the Auld Holland Inn, in Oak Harbor. This otherwise undistinguished building has a huge plastic windmill stuck on the top, for no apparent reason other than to match the name. It had been suggested to me that cycling across the USA would be quite boring: miles and miles of long straight roads with nothing much to look at. But although relatively short at just over sixty miles, the first day's route had been full of interest. It even had a plastic windmill. And somehow, we had packed in over 5000 feet of ascent. The red-hot weather had helped with the holiday mood, and the whole day had felt like a gentle sightseeing trip. Even now, although the heat was decreasing a little, our freshly-washed cycle kit baked dry in minutes. As we sat contentedly in the local Chinese restaurant early that evening we reflected on a superb first day, and tried not to think about the implications for future daily mileages of only completing 67 miles on day one, nor the fact that we were still considerably to the west of Seattle.

We must have been more tired that we realised, because we slept right through the din of the July 4th fireworks display that was starting just as we retired early to bed. At breakfast, our fellow guests were astonished and, I think, slightly offended, to find that we hadn't stayed up to see any of it. Apparently, it was the best for years. But we were men on a mission, and we both knew that the keys to success were good food and good sleep, and we were not to be distracted from either. I certainly was not about to admit that the xenophobic bill boards beside the road yesterday proclaiming 'No aid for Syria. What about us?' and 'America First', and the proximity of a large naval air base whose entrance was covered with military jingoism, had not helped me buy in to the patriotic mood that had surrounded the preparations for the big night. So, the goal that morning was to avoid political conversation, to eat as much motel breakfast as possible, and to smuggle a suitable supply of cakes and bananas into our back pockets for later. Mission accomplished.

We crossed to Fidalgo Island, the final one in the chain, by way of Deception Pass. This is another of those sea passages that is nowadays crossed by a bridge; in this case, since 1935, by two beautiful, curving steel structures, high above the water, using tiny Pass Island as a stepping stone. This is also another sea passage that the Vancouver expedition failed to find, at least first time around. They were an incompetent lot, those early explorers. The name commemorates the mistake. For us, this was another delightful place to linger and to take photos. A very narrow pedestrian footpath was perched perilously above the 150-foot drop to the sea below. On another perfect blue-sky morning, the whirlpools created by the huge tidal race through the narrow channel looked enchanting – and it was entertaining to watch the power boats fight their way through the surf. Nowadays the place is a marine nature reserve, with a diverse array of marine life enjoying the oxygen rich waters. But the area has a grim history. In the 1880s, Ben Ure Island, just to the east, was infamous as a base for the highly profitable human smuggling of migrant Chinese people for labour. The United States Customs Department was on to it, and for years Ben Ure and his fellow smugglers played hide-and-seek with the customs. Being caught in the act meant execution, so Ure would tie the migrant people up in burlap bags so that, if customs agents were to approach, then he could easily toss them overboard. The tidal currents would carry the drowned migrants' bodies through Deception Pass towards San Juan Island to the north and west, where many ended up in what became known as Dead Man's Bay.

On Fidalgo Island, Highway 20 became bigger, and the traffic levels began to pick up as we approached the main north-south coastal corridor. So, we turned off onto minor roads around the shore of Similk Bay, past more picture postcard settlements of white clapboard houses, with the mandatory veranda and manicured lawns. Only these were not 'historic', but newly built and gigantic, usually with a boat house attached. More Amazon executives, no doubt. We crossed the Swinomish Channel to the mainland on a final high bridge and called in at La Connor, to begin what was to become another great tradition of the trip – the second breakfast. The problem was that we were staying in very cheap motels where the breakfast, if provided at all, was barely adequate for normal people, never mind anyone trying to cycle 100 miles a day. There was usually cereal – but a belly full of milk and soggy, cardboard-like pulp is a pretty disastrous way to start the day. Sometimes we could get porridge in a plastic bag, just add boiling water, sometimes overcooked bacon, and rubberised eggs, sometimes fruit, usually small cakes in plastic bags and, of course, coffee. But after an hour or two of cycling we were starving. Given that we were away at 8 o'clock most mornings, the solution was a second breakfast at a café or roadside diner between 9 and 10 o'clock. Perfect. This was a Sunday morning in La Connor, and the Calico Cupboard Café was packed with people recovering from fireworks parties the night before. We had to wait, but it was worth it for the maple and bacon cake, with sugar icing.

Leaving La Connor, we had a short taste of flat ground as we crossed the Skagit river delta. But the pleasure was offset by the frustration of trying to make diagonal progress across a square grid pattern of roads. It turns out that there are no short cuts, as we were to appreciate more fully once we reached the Great Plains. As we crossed the floodplain, the Cascades mountains reared up ahead in a seemingly impregnable wall. The plan was to follow the Skagit river valley, deep into the mountains, but there was precious little sign of it from here. The entrance must be very narrow. We joined a local traffic-free cycle route but, as so often, regretted it within minutes and returned in despair to the road. Who designs and builds these useless efforts? This one cut through a grid of residential streets on the edge of Mount Vernon, each street just a few hundred yards apart. The surface was dreadful. At each junction, every few seconds, we were forced to give way to traffic, without crossing lights or any marking on the road. There were no proper dropped kerbs. Whereas, on the parallel road, we just sailed through without stopping. Why would anyone use such a bike path? With the honourable exception of Holland and, perhaps, Belgium, it's been the same wherever I have cycled.

The afternoon brought a change of gear in the cycling, as we found the entrance to the Skagit Valley and rode a

30-mile section of valley road, running alongside the river. Highway 20, with all the traffic, was on the other bank. We had the minor road to ourselves, with great views of the sinuous curves of the river, and a light tailwind. For the first time, Tim and I began to hit a smooth rhythm, working together by riding one behind the other and taking turns on the front, where the air resistance makes for much harder work. Sheltering in second place gives an opportunity to recover from an effort on the front, but failure to 'come through' and take the lead again quickly leads to friction between cyclists. Knowing that the American roads would often be long and straight, and knowing my propensity to daydream on a bicycle and to lose track of time, I had decided on a novel solution to a problem that had not yet arisen. I had attached a tiny, light weight, electronic egg timer to the top of the little tank bag, behind my handlebar stem. This was the perfect time to test it out. As Tim hit the front, so I hit the button. Three minutes later .... "tring, tring, tring" ... it was time to change over and to hit the button again. Three minutes later .... "tring, tring, tring" ... and all change once more. I was delighted with the stunning success of this innovation, and I can't remember 30 miles ever going past so quickly before. Justice, and world peace in our time. And such entertainment! I looked forward to patenting the idea and making a small fortune.

Crossing the Skagit river again, a gigantic, rippled wall of concrete welcomed us to the town of Concrete, in letters about 50 feet tall. This was a company town, belonging to the Portland Cement Company, and the giant ripples were the cylindrical, conjoined towers of an old flour mill. We learnt that the slogan had been painted for the 1993, De Niro film, 'This Boy's Life'. In town, we found the Concrete Drug Store - concrete drugs can't be good for you - and the Concrete Theatre where, presumably, no imagination is required. The heat was intense, so we sat in the shade and refilled ourselves and our water bottles with copious amounts of iced water for the final leg.

We ended the day at the Skagit River Resort, where we had a peaceful cabin in the woods, miles from anywhere. Deer strolled through the garden. Butterflies sniffed out our washing as it dried on the line. Tame rabbits wandered around outside, and inside if we left the door open. The Resort motto is 'You're no bunny 'til some bunny loves you!' Tim enjoyed himself trying to get close-up, rabbits-eye-view pictures of some of the most photogenic bunnies, but I don't think love was in the air.

2 THE CASCADES AND THE WASHINGTON PLATEAU

The next morning the owners were kind enough to open 'The Eatery' early. We wanted to be over the five and a half thousand-foot-high, Washington Pass before the temperature soared. This time the first breakfast was the real deal, and we put away enormous quantities of bacon, eggs, and pancakes, all with generous helpings of maple syrup. This was just as well because, when we reached the last village in the valley, Newhalem, at 8.30 we found that the general store didn't open until 10.00. We had no food or water, having planned to fill up there. We hung around for a while, photographing each other in front of an old steam locomotive. Newhalem was another company town, this one owned by the Seattle Light Company and inhabited entirely by the staff of the next-door hydro plant (whose dam came courtesy of concrete from Concrete). Two women arrived and entered the store, but they weren't prepared to sell us anything. It was 60 miles and around 7000 feet of climbing over the Rainy and Washington Passes to the next supplies. Being rash, impatient, and concerned about the heat, we set off

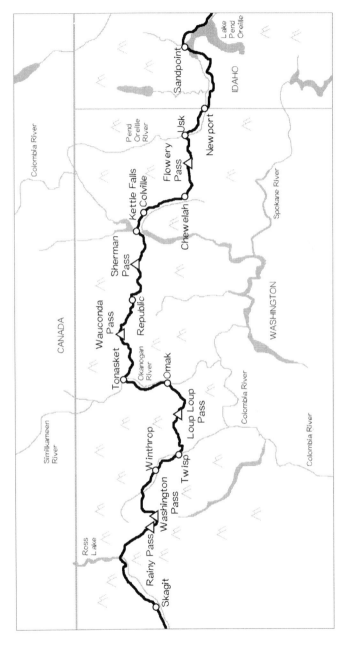

regardless, and did the whole thing 'pan y agua' as the cyclists say when they're not using drugs. Except, in our case, without the bread either, and using water from snowmelt in mountain streams. Don't try this at home, children.

We entered the Diablo Gorge, where the road began to climb properly for the first time. Spectacular cliffs gave way to a short road tunnel, and then we were looking down on Gorge Lake, the first of a series of hydro lakes built between 1937 and the 1950s. We had seen this section of the route from the air during our descent to Seattle, so the bridge that takes the road diagonally across the lake seemed strangely familiar as we crossed it. A road over the Washington Pass was planned from at least 1885, and it seems amazing to think that the North Cascades Highway was not completed until 1972, so difficult was the terrain up through the Diablo Gorge and beyond. Flash floods in the gorge tore out early attempts at road building, and avalanches took out later ones. Before 1972, this was a pristine wilderness, with native Americans having used the route for around 8000 years as a link between Washington State's eastern plateau and the sea. Even now, the road is closed between November and April because of the depth of snow and, more particularly, the extreme danger of avalanches. And we were about to ride over it in summer clothes, with no food or water.

We set off in high spirits, stopping after a few miles to pose for an unmissable photo opportunity in front of a mountain called Thunder Knob. Positioning the caption on our blogs was done very carefully. Soon we caught up with the first touring cyclists we had seen since leaving Seattle, a middle-aged couple crawling up the pass on ridiculously heavily-laden bikes. We shouted encouragement as we sped by on our lightweight thoroughbreds, feeling smug. (Since Einstein, speed has been a relative concept, though smugness is absolute). After an hour or so, the gradient steepened significantly, although we were nowhere near the summit. It was already very hot. We stopped to fill our bottles from a waterfall spilling over a roadside crag. Before leaving Seattle, we had taken the precaution of posting ahead supplies of our favourite gels and energy drink powders. We had brought them all the way from home, and we sent them to hotels a few days apart along our route. Getting sachets of white powder through Seattle airport had proved interesting, but they let us go eventually. However, the first batch was in our tiny luggage bags, and this was bordering on an emergency. Fuelled by a week's supply of energy gels, consumed in one go, we shot up the mountain.

The top of the Rainy Pass was bone dry, fortunately, and just above the tree line. Alpine meadows, criss-crossed by gushing, meltwater streams soared upwards to the foot of huge cliffs that led, in turn, to jagged, snow-capped ridges and rock spires, and the perfect blue sky above. A magnificent sight. A fast descent of nearly ten minutes led to the final long climb up to the Washington Pass. Our blood sugar levels were dropping fast as we struggled up the final slopes. But the views from the top were, if anything, even better than the Rainy Pass. We stopped for trophy photographs underneath the signboard: 'Washington Pass, 5477 feet'. To our right were the vertical rock walls of Liberty Bell Mountain, a rock climber's paradise of top quality granite. The most popular route is, of course, called Liberty Bell Crack.

Tim and I have enjoyed rock climbing together over the years, the highlight of which was a memorable trip to the Italian Dolomites, where the cliffs were possibly even taller. We stared upwards with our mouths watering, trying to locate Liberty Bell Crack. We had first met over twenty years ago, when our children were at the same junior school. I was new to the area and was looking for a partner for hill walking trips to Scotland. Summer walking led to winter trips, and the development of winter climbing skills. We also began to rock climb in summer, and before I knew it, after leaving the Fire Service, Tim had become a fully-fledged mountaineer, going on to complete the highest summits on all seven continents. Yes, that includes Everest. Once I had become fixated on the idea of cycling across the States on a lightweight bike, on a schedule of 100-miles-a-day, Tim was the natural choice of partner in crime. Besides, no one else was daft enough to come with me.

"Road bikes won't stand up to the punishment", the rest said. "You can't go that light".

But not Tim.

I remember asking him, because it was a couple of weeks after I had had a heart pacemaker fitted, at the tender age of 54. We were out on the bikes together, with me road-testing my newly-fitted electronic control system. Partly, it was to distract from the pain in my shoulder, as rock hard tyres and a finely tuned carbon-fibre frame transmitted every bump, crack, and pothole of the decaying, North Yorkshire road surface, straight up my left arm to the wound over my new pacemaker. Partly, it was a statement of defiance in the face of intimations of mortality.

"Tim. I'm planning to ride across America, from Seattle to Boston. It's 4000 miles so, to make it interesting, I'm aiming for 40 days".

I could hear the cogs whirring.

"That's 100 miles a day" I added, helpfully. "So, light weight, on fast road bikes, using cheap motels. Do you want to come?"

Tim's eyes lit up at the prospect of another challenge and the reply was immediate.

"Sounds great. Yes, of course!"

After all, what do you do after the Seven Summits? Having Tim's indomitable spirit alongside me was exactly what I needed. Although it was also slightly intimidating to know that Tim was not about to give up, no matter what the circumstances, and I would need to match his determination when things got tough.

What goes up must come down, and so we began a screaming descent down the broad hairpin underneath Liberty Bell Spire. This was the point where the winter avalanches thunder across the road, crossing it twice as the road hairpins back on itself. The evidence was all around, in the form of crushed trees, huge boulders and piles of earth and rock debris bulldozed from the road during the spring, road-opening process. In what seemed like just a few minutes we hurtled down three and a half thousand feet in twenty miles to reach the tiny hamlet of Mazama. The general store had a café, and it absorbed the full force of our hunger. After the equivalent of several lunches each, we finished off with a monster slice of Blueberry Pie, the first of the trip and, I think, unsurpassed by any of the Blueberry Pies that followed. A final, gentle roll down the Methow valley brought us to Winthrop.

Winthrop sells itself as a wild west town, and 'The Virginian' was filmed here, so you get the picture. No white paint, just utilitarian, brown wooden buildings with verandas for shelter from snow and sun, and hitching rails for your horse. Unfortunately, there was a line of pickup trucks parked where the horses should have been. I think it's called progress.

While wandering around the town we met a friendly, holidaying family who were intrigued by our jerseys. The sharp eyed young lad not only did the mental arithmetic correctly, but he figured out from the map that we were planning to cycle right through their home town of Richmond, in Michigan state. Dad, Greg, was a keen cyclist and he offered to ride his local section with us, since the family will be back from holiday by then. I saw an opportunity to check a navigational detail.

"Is the Bluewater ferry across the St Clair River still

running?" I asked. "It's just that the website seems out of date".

Clearly Greg had not been expecting to meet an English cyclist in Washington State with a detailed knowledge of the geography of his corner of south east Michigan. But, once he had recovered from the shock, Greg reassured us that the ferry is still running, and soon we were immersed in a discussion of the best dining options in Marine City. The truth was that I had spent a huge amount of time, over the years, immersed in the detailed planning our route and I had pretty much memorised the whole thing.

Our route from Seattle to Boston is not the quickest or the most direct. That honour goes to a combination of Interstates 90 and 94. Together, they link the cities in just 3,051 miles. Our 4000-mile route is the result of weaving together all the places in the northern USA that I really wanted to see: Washington coast and the big passes of Washington state; back country Montana; Yellowstone Park (as much of it as possible); the Black Hills; the Badlands National Park; the Mississippi River; the Great Lakes; Niagara Falls; Five Finger Lakes; the Adirondacks; Lake Champlain; and the Green Mountains. There is an 'official' Northern Tier cycle route, and various companies offer guided crossings at exorbitant prices, but none of these routes pull together everything that I wanted. Mine requires a certain amount of looping around to make it work, and my one regret was that we still had to miss out Glacier National Park, but I still consider the finished route a thing of beauty.

Our hotel was on the far side of town, so after the navigational chat, we were back on the bikes. After a few minutes, my faithful bicycle GPS brought us to a halt right outside a hotel. The problem was that it was not the hotel I had booked. We rode up and down in increasing frustration, looking for the right one, until I grasped the nettle and marched in to reception.

"Oh", they said, "That's what we used to be called until we changed the name".

GPS, one: hotel communications team, zero.

After dinner, back in the centre of Winthrop, we found an elevated terrace from which to watch the world go by. Soon we spied two familiar shapes moving slowly down the main street below, as the sun began to set. It was our friends on the heavy touring bikes, fully six hours behind us. The woman was right at the end of her strength, and they still had to find somewhere to camp. They too were planning to cycle across the whole country and, having seen us fly past, they now began to list all the items that they intended to ditch before carrying on. It certainly looked as though they needed to do so. But we had all crossed the first great geographical hurdle, the Cascades, and a different looking country lay ahead.

Cycling down the Methow Valley towards Twisp, the following morning, we had our first experience of the sheer variety of the scenery of the USA, and the speed of transition from one geographic zone to the next. Yesterday's lush and spectacular alpine scenery had vanished. In place of the rock spires, dense woods, and alpine meadows, there was an altogether more arid landscape, with fewer trees, and rolling hills. Crossing the Cascades had brought a distinct change in the colour palette too; from intense green forest under pure blue skies, to ochre-coloured grassy slopes and a hazy, steel-grey sky. Forest fires to the south of us were spewing smoke into the high atmosphere, where it was blotting out the sun, but not lowering the temperature significantly.

Twisp was also a very different kind of place from any we'd seen before. This was a small, remote working town, not a posh commuter village, and certainly not a tourist hotspot like Winthrop. We rode up and down the dusty main street, looking for somewhere for a second breakfast. Many shops were boarded up, and there were several frontages that looked as though they offered agricultural or engineering services, but their exact purpose we could only guess at. Close examination revealed a diner with signs of life. The interior was distinctly utilitarian, no chalkboards here, and an old man sat on a wooden bench, reading the paper. Tim's opening gambit was to ask for a cappuccino, but this was a mistake. The woman behind the counter scowled at us.

"We only have regular cawfee, none of your fancy cappuccinos".

The final, distasteful word was spat out, with venom. Luckily, they also served regular bacon, eggs, and pancakes. We were learning the hard way that there really is a deep cultural divide between the America of posh coffee shops, and its working heartlands, something that was driven home repeatedly as we travelled east. Somehow, we had crossed a cultural divide that was every bit as real as the geographical one.

Climbing the Loup Loup pass, we had our first encounter with a gigantic, fully laden timber truck, careering down the narrow, but beautifully engineered curves. These trucks stop for no one. One moment we'd be enjoying the peace and tranquillity of a remote, almost car-free, mountain road, and seconds later we'd be recovering from a near death experience. The blind bends were a game of two-wheeled Russian roulette, and the truck drivers were not going to lose.

We didn't cut any corners on the descent that took us into the Okanagan valley, where orchards of apple trees adorned the upper slopes. Acres of silvery netting, viewed through a smoke haze, looked very strange. Tim stopped in the road for an arty photograph, managing to complete the surreal shot by finding a field of abandoned, rusting helicopters for the foreground. Fortunately, the shutter clicked just before the thunder of wheels announced the arrival of the latest timber truck, and the driver just missed the chance to take him out.

Every small town needs its entertainment, and in Omak they have the 'World Famous Omak Suicide Race'. No, I'd never heard of it either. It turns out to be a rodeo race, but at the extreme end of the spectrum, so animal rights activists should look away now. The ice-age sediment on the valley floor is so thick that, over time, the massive Okanagan river has carved its way deep into the boulder clay. At a bend in the river, opposite the rodeo ground, the soft earth of the river bank is fully 200 feet high, at an angle of about 60 degrees. Perfect for a Suicide Race. Every August, about 50 horses and riders take a short run up, and then hurtle straight over the edge, plunging 200 feet down the bank into the river. Any survivors then swim across, race to the Rodeo ground, and the first one to complete a lap is the winner. Having arrived too early in the summer, I was sad that we had to make do with video of previous races, posted on the internet. Or did we? We found the site, and peered over the edge of what is one hell of a big, steep drop! The river tore at the bank as it shot round the curve, far beneath us. Of course, if we had brought mountain bikes with us then we'd have had a go, but not on these thoroughbred Bianchis. They can't swim.

We retreated, and found a chicken salad in a very smart, air-conditioned café, full of well-heeled ladies-who-lunch. We were back to fancy coffee. Stepping out of the door afterwards was like walking into a blast furnace. I remember once changing planes at Doha airport, and the wind coming off the Arabian desert was refreshingly cool compared to this. The 20 miles to Tonasket were the hottest I have ever cycled. We set off with bottles full of iced water but, within minutes, the water was hot enough to make tea. The egg timer came into its own again, as we took three-minute turns on the front, battling the red-hot headwind. It turned out that three minutes was exactly right, if you wanted to have runny bits left in the middle.

Another minute and we would have been hard boiled, that's for sure.

Tonasket had a 24-hour gas station with super-cold air conditioning, and that's all I can tell you about the place. I certainly wasn't going back outside. The thermometer said 105F, and that's 40C. I worked my way happily through outsized paper buckets of luridly-coloured iced drinks, dispensed from gargantuan machines. Next door was a very basic motel, offering room only, and our home for the night. The whole thing was cunningly arranged so that drivers never had to take more than four or five steps from car to gas station shop, or car to motel room. For many of them, this was a serious challenge that had nothing to do with the temperature. Getting out from behind the steering wheel was the first problem. I thought we were going to have to call the fire department for a woman, probably around 25 stone, who appeared to be completely stuck. She wriggled and squirmed and wheezed for ages before freeing herself. Then there was the descent from cab to ground level, when overhanging flesh made it hard to spot the ground, and underpowered legs hardly looked up to the job. And then, there was walking. Let's just say that bipedal locomotion did not seem the obvious evolutionary solution for these body shapes, and it was hard to understand why rolling had not evolved instead. But I shouldn't be too rude. When we weren't pedalling, our lifestyle became equally sedentary, carbohydrate and sugar rich. We called it recovery, and spent the afternoon reading, sleeping, and updating blogs.

Extreme weather called for extreme measures. We were up before 5am, back in the gas station trying to put together something resembling the kind of breakfast that might get us over the Wauconda Pass, the first of two huge passes for the day. It was only just daylight, and deliciously cool. The 6% grade started right outside the motel and led up through arid scrubland, to high, irrigated valleys where the main crop appeared to be fodder grass. Further up, we entered steeper, forested ground, and stopped for snacks on a section of hairpins. Flat ground was hard to find, so we sat on the tarmac, on the shoulder of the road, on the outside of a bend. This turned out to be the perfect place for close-up, ground level, action photos of logging trucks hurtling down the mountain. And an even better spot for taking action shots of your cycling partner doing stupid things with a camera, right in the path of logging trucks hurtling down the mountain. Our ears were still ringing from the indignant airhorns as we got back on the bikes, grinning wildly. There are some mornings when it's good to be alive!

We were over the Wauconda Pass and down to Republic for 9.30am, and a celebratory second breakfast. Republic is another proper wild west town, dating from the gold rush in the 1890s. But the mining was very short lived and nowadays, apart from the period shopfronts, there are but two attractions: a fossil hunting centre and – wait for it – a wooden carousel built in 1896, and one of the oldest in the USA. But, after the thrills and spills of motor-sport, live-action photography, these pastimes seemed rather tame, so we left them to the families of holiday makers who were just starting to arrive.

The Sherman Pass was our highest point so far. We climbed steeply up through rolling, grass covered hills with individual conifer trees dotted all over the landscape. I'd only ever seen scenery like this in Westerns, so this was a real treat. At the top, a group of exhausted-looking cyclists were worrying about the atmospheric smoke; would it damage their lungs, and would the fires close their roads? Our light-hearted attempts at banter had no effect whatsoever. Let's just say there was a mismatch in moods, so we left them to it and shot off down the other side.

But there was one minor niggle that was beginning to

frustrate Tim. The canny roadbuilders had so far succeeded in keeping the gradients on all the passes to a steady 6-8%, as measured by our on-board Garmins. This was fine for going up, but on the fast descents, once you could no longer pedal, it made for a terminal velocity that was frustratingly close to 50 mph, but not quite there. Having hit 48.8 mph the previous day, and 49.5 mph earlier that morning, Tim was determined to hit 50 mph this time. Let me admit, right away, that this is one competition that I am never going to win, largely because I struggle to keep my weight up towards 10 stones, and Tim is 3 stone heavier than me. Judging by the fact that we cycle uphill at much the same speed, our power-to-weight ratios are probably quite similar, although that's no consolation when you consider what it says about my meagre power output! Over the years, I have grown used to watching helplessly as Tim, and other cycling mates, freewheel slowly away from me on long descents. I can contort myself into the most painfully aerodynamic tuck positions known to humanity, but I still get dropped. The only chance I have is to grab Tim's wheel as he rolls over the summit, to get sucked along in the vortex right behind him. I can tell you that, doing very nearly 50 mph lined up only a couple of feet from Tim's rear wheel and with no view of the twisting descent ahead, is very exciting, and requires a lot of trust in Tim's cornering skills! And all to no avail this time, as we just missed out again.

Kettle Falls, on the mighty Colombia River is a sad sort of place. This magnificent series of rapids and big waterfalls had been a major salmon fishing site, sustaining native American peoples from a wide area since ancient times. The river had carved huge, semi-spherical chambers, or kettles, into the quartzite bedrock below the falls, and these were said to be so packed with salmon in the summer spawning season that you could walk across the river. There are photographs of elaborate, wooden, scaffolding structures used to cantilever netting out over the river to catch the leaping salmon in mid-air. Fishing here was dangerous, because of the rushing water and slippery rocks, and required a high degree of organization. A salmon chief, or 'Chief of the Waters', opened the season by spearing the first fish. Fishermen speared and netted up to 3,000 fish in a single day. But all this ended abruptly in 1940, when the completion of the Grand Coulee Dam for hydroelectric power created the 150-mile-long Lake Roosevelt and flooded the falls under 90 feet of water. On June 14th that year, as the waters rose, around 8000 members of tribes from all over the Northwest gathered at Kettle Falls for a three-day 'Ceremony of Tears' to mourn the loss of their ancestral fishing grounds. All that remains today are a pair of ugly, steel-girder bridges for a rail and road crossing, high above the sullen grey waters. It was quite sobering, and the exhilaration of the descent from the Sherman Pass evaporated as we crossed over, and climbed up the far bank to the relocated town of Kettle Falls. Still, this was our first major river crossing, and a tangible sign of easterly progress.

On the edge of Kettle Falls were a wood-fired power station and an enormous plywood factory. We had found logging-truck Mecca. In fact, the road was now so busy with these huge trucks that we bottled out of cycling the narrow roadway on the Kettle Falls bridge. Trucks travelling in opposite directions at high speed only just squeezed passed each other, hemmed in by the steel-girder superstructure. Two trucks and a cyclist were not going to fit. Whilst meeting a cyclist on the bridge might possibly have slowed the trucks down, it would only be in the same way that a speed hump would slow them. And that's assuming they weren't looking for payback after our antics on the Wauconda Pass earlier that morning. Luckily, a narrow pedestrian walkway on one side of the bridge gave us safe passage, and a stopping point for photos.

Whilst downing the usual litres of garishly-coloured iced liquid in a gas station in Kettle Falls, we spied our first

Hummer. This is the civilian version of the Humvee, the High Mobility Multipurpose Wheeled Vehicle, beloved of the United States military, and prominent in the 1991 Gulf War. I parked my Bianchi Infinito CV next to it, for comparative purposes, and here are the key numbers:

- Weight: 2,900 kg versus 7.3 kg
- Length: 5.168 versus 1.73 meters
- Width: 2.197 versus 0.42 meters
- Fuel consumption: 9 mpg versus 23 miles per breakfast
- Top speed: 98 versus 49.5 mph (so far, but we hadn't yet found a seriously steep descent)

Hummers make the perfect all-American family vehicle. Their huge size and weight means you can threaten other drivers just by being on the move, and they are impossible to park anywhere except in the middle of the carriageway, right outside your destination. Since the Hummer is a Class 3 truck, you don't have to bother with any safety regulations or safety features, no child locks, child seat tethers, side air bags, or stability control. And, for your trophy cabinet, Hummer drivers receive about five times as many traffic tickets as the national average for all vehicles. Fantastic.

Somehow, I preferred the Bianchi Infinito CVs that we were each riding. At the start of the trip, we had woken, jetlagged and very early, in a twin room in Seattle, to find the still-almost-brand-new bikes that we had bought for the trip, sitting in cardboard boxes at the foot of our beds. It had brought back happy memories of childhood Christmas mornings with my brothers. We had spent a couple of hours contentedly unpacking, rebuilding, inflating the tyres, and polishing the carbon fibre until it gleamed. These bikes are perfect for long days in the saddle. They have a slightly more 'relaxed' geometry than my road race bike (the riding position is a little more upright), but the best feature is the 'countervail' technology that Bianchi has built into the carbon fibre frame to dampen vibration from the road. I was sceptical at first, but it really is superb. This is the most comfortable bike I have ever ridden. I didn't have a moment's discomfort, despite all the hours in the saddle. The only concession to transcontinental travel that we made, was to change the tyres for heavier, but bomb-proof, four season Continentals. The shoulders of the roads, where we usually cycled, were covered in an unattractive assortment of scrap metal, glass, rubble, dead animals, and pieces of wood, and these tyres coped manfully with the lot. The only item that defeated them were the small pieces of wire from the side walls of decaying tyres, helpfully shed in vast quantities by the ubiquitous logging trucks. If we were lucky, shreds of black rubber, still attached, were enough to alert us to the danger. But fully shredded wires were invisible, and the sharp ends were more than enough to puncture even these Kevlar reinforced tyres. I think we had three such punctures in the first few days, whilst mixing it with the logging trucks. But once out of their territory, apart from a high speed, front wheel snakebite, courtesy of a Yellowstone Park pothole (that's a compression double puncture, no snakes involved, but probably just as dangerous), and Tim's ten-mile stutter on the first morning (almost certainly the result of pinching the inner tube when he re-inflated the tyre on 'Christmas' morning), we came through unscathed.

Colville had a modern, sprawling, non-descript hotel, on the edge of town, surrounded by fast food outlets to match. So far, we had been able to bring our bikes safely into all the hotel rooms, and it was the same here. 'Recovery' meant that we weren't prepared to walk far, so the long, straight, ground floor corridor leading to our room was perfect. Once out of sight of the receptionist, we could pedal all the way to our room. But the strict rules of 'recovery' also meant not venturing into town in the evening, but making do with the next-door Pizza Hut for our meal. This wasn't ideal, given that we needed high levels of protein to match the carbs, and we resolved to do better in the future. But our visit to Pizza Hut continued our cultural education. The place had about 20 huge TV screens, side by side, just above head height, right around the 360 degrees of wall. Most were showing different channels, so it was possible to watch a football match at the same time as the news, a game show, a baseball match, and a couple of films. Imagine the brainpower needed to process that lot simultaneously. We scanned the room, looking for evidence of such intellectual giants. Well, they were certainly giants. The family of four, next to us, had a combined weight of well over 60 stones, and the kids were not more than 10 years old. This was the other America, where restaurants don't have chalkboards and fancy coffee, and where there are fixed benches on which you could park a Humvee, rather than conventional chairs, whose legs wouldn't stand a chance.

The amazing thing was that, in the morning, we only needed to ride the 24, fast and easy miles down the valley to Chewelah, for our second breakfast, to find the epitome of a 'posh-coffee', fairly-traded, wholefood café. This breakfast cost us about twice as much as most others, despite having only half the calories, and the customers were only half the size. We were greeted by a woman who said she had overtaken us in her car, leaving Colville, just over an hour earlier. She could not get her head round the fact that, by the time she had parked, shopped, and wandered across to the café, we were only a few minutes behind her. People have no idea of what is possible on a bicycle – particularly, as in this case, downhill, with a tailwind.

Sadly, such ideal conditions never last long, and soon

we were climbing the last of the 'warm-up' passes on our mammoth route. The Flowery Pass was not noticeably flowery, but it was a delightful climb up a quiet side road. Life really doesn't get much better than this. It was a lovely, hot day, and as we left the café, we had 2500 feet of climbing to look forward to, in great scenery, and we still had weeks of this ahead. There was disappointment on the descent though, because the 50 mph barrier eluded Tim again, and there wouldn't be another chance for quite a while.

The Pend Orielle river was idyllic, which was just as well, because we'd be following it, and the Clark Fork, upstream, for a couple of days. Crossing the bridge at Usk, we left Highway 20 in favour of a quiet side road on the far bank. The river was full of old wooden posts, used to attach salmon nets, and the whole scene was as relaxed and peaceful as my mood. As the morning heat began to increase, we ran between recently cut grass meadows, where an ominous whirring sound began, followed shortly by sharp impacts to the legs, body, face, and cycle helmet. We had run into a cloud of locusts. The internet tells me that the huge, Rocky Mountain Locust, that decimated crops in the 1880s, is extinct, so it probably wasn't those. I think these were Carolina locusts, and they were quite big enough for me. Most were sunning themselves on the hot tarmac, or flying at low level, and our spokes began to ping musically with diced locust. There didn't seem to be anything to be gained by stopping, so we pushed on fast, hands over mouths to prevent accidental ingestion. Chains and sprockets began to clog up with mangled corpses, and then, suddenly, we were out of the other side. We stopped to clean the bikes and drive chains with a rag, and made the unexpected discovery that locust juice is an excellent, all-purpose, bicycle lubricant. With the locust exoskeletons wiped from the outside, the chains just purred round, and they didn't need reoiling for days.

Things were becoming very Welsh. The next town

upriver from Usk was Newport, and here we entered Idaho, our second state. Our lunchtime chicken salad was taken on an air-conditioned restaurant terrace, with a great view out over the river. As always, the shirts caused quite a stir. The waiter wanted to know,

"What are you doing it for?"

This was another of the questions that we were becoming very used to. To begin with, I had taken this as my cue to hold forth on the deep, existential questions of transcontinental cycling, such as, 'Why cycle it, when you could fly across in three hours?' But I soon learnt that what they really meant was a lot more specific: 'Which charity are you raising money for?'

At this point, Tim explained to the waiter that he was raising money for Yorkshire Cancer Research. I was in two minds about this. On the one hand, I was grateful for the way in which this response seemed to convince people that we might, possibly, be sane, after all. It smoothed some difficult, interpersonal moments. And some people, including the waiter in Newport, made generous contributions to a worthwhile cause. But most of me resented the way in which the journey was assumed to have no value, unless it made money for someone. And I hated the equivalence between bike-riding and fund-raising, as though it's the only reason for getting on a bike. To my shame, I never plucked up the courage to say,

"I'm just doing it for the hell of it", but I certainly wanted to.

In the afternoon, we entered an area of mixed forest, farmsteads, pastureland, and small lakes. Still on minor roads, we pedalled along quietly, just enjoying the heat and the views. A huge, white headed, bird of prey was perched on a telegraph pole. It wasn't a bald eagle, but despite some good photos, we never identified it. Having been fooled previously by dummies, designed to scare birds from the crops, I can assure you that this one was real. It flew off.

Sandpoint was our largest town since Seattle, and the approach was across Lake Pend Oreille, on a causeway bridge on stilts, about a mile long. A spectacular way to make an entrance. No boring, out-of-town motel for us this time, and instead we checked into a very twee bed and breakfast. Blue painted clapboard, veranda, rocking chairs, and chintz. Sandpoint was home to the first microbrewery that we had seen since leaving Seattle. In fact, the beer on the road up to that point had been disappointing, so we were looking forward to some interesting local brews. The brewery had its own pub, serving an impressive array of beers and, to our delight, top quality steaks. Our protein crisis was solved. As someone who had only ever eaten shoe-leather steaks in the UK, these were a revelation. Succulent and juicy, matched with local IPA, they were the perfect antidote to our first 100-mile day in the saddle. We even had energy left over to seek out the beach at the head of the lake, where we promenaded with a long line of geese, and watched the sun set in the smoky haze of the forest fires.

3 MONTANA

Sandpoint was the trigger point of the Missoula floods. These were cataclysmic, ice-age events that left enormous scars all over the landscape of the north-western states. This whole area was at the southern edge of an ice cap that lay over Canada and the northern part of the USA. A glacier projected south towards Sandpoint, down what is now the Kootenay valley. As it moved southwards, it blocked the course of the Clark Fork River. Upstream, this river was hemmed in by mountains on its south flank, and the ice to its north. Having nowhere to go, the water backed up behind the glacial, ice dam at Sandpoint, forming a huge lake, known as Missoula Lake. You may be surprised to learn that Missoula is nearly 200 miles from Sandpoint, but Missoula was, indeed, the centre of the vast lake, that was around 2000 feet deep. It backed up another 200 miles or so, beyond Missoula, to the south east. But it's what happened next that is the most spectacular. The ice dam failed suddenly, triggering the release of the entire lake in a single, gargantuan, outpouring of water. It's been calculated that the wall of escaping water travelled south westwards at up to 80 mph, scouring out the distinctive canyons of 'The Badlands', and the gorge behind Portland, now occupied by the Colombia river, before escaping to the sea. At its peak, the flow rate was 9.5 cubic miles an hour, or 60 times that of the Amazon today. Strangest of all, geologists believe that this was repeated many times during the ice age, as the collapsed glacier regrew, blocked the river, and then failed again. The modern lake at Sandpoint is the last, pathetic puddle.

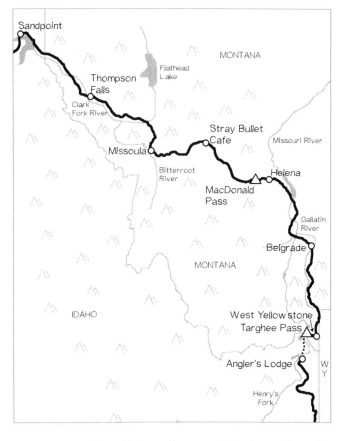

Next morning, all the talk was of the forest fires that were out of control in remote country a few miles to the south. We watched helicopters scooping water out of the lake before they wheeled away towards the fires. For us, the first few miles out of town were very busy with traffic. This was a pattern that we grew to recognise. It seems that most people live not in town, but very close to it, and they all use their cars back and forth for everything. For 5 to 10 miles around towns, the roads can be very busy, but in the gaps in between – and these can often be 50 miles or more – the roads are deserted. Guess which we preferred. As the traffic thinned out, we came back to the lake shore, travelling round it clockwise. I'm sorry. It's not a pathetic puddle at all, but rather majestic in scale, and very beautiful, close-up, where its flooded, woodland fringes harbour important wild life reserves. David Thompson, the first European to reach the shores of the lake in 1809, promptly built a cabin and stayed put, in splendid isolation, for years. As we passed the site of his memorial, we could see why. It's a lovely spot.

A rail road track came through Sandpoint, and round the lake in the same direction as we were travelling. We had our first sighting of the immensely long freight trains that, very slowly, criss-cross the country. The rail line repeatedly cut corners, bypassing inconvenient bays and inlets on an embankment far out in the lake. We lingered and managed to get some great photos of these immense trains, apparently hovering above the water.

Leaving the lake, we entered Montana, after less than 100 miles across the 'panhandle' of Idaho, to which we would return later. We followed the deeply-incised, Clark Fork river valley towards Missoula, in my imagination, travelling upstream against the unleashed mega-torrent. After yesterday's exertions in varied country, this rolling, dead straight, road through the forest held less appeal, and was a more serious strain on the legs. There were very few houses, never mind villages, and the egg timer came out again, extended to 5-minute turns to reflect the expanded distances between stops.

Trout Creek had only three buildings, but one of them

was a big log cabin that said 'Diner', so that was good enough for us. There were only a couple of cars outside, and it looked as though it might be closed. But the door opened to reveal a single, gloomy room, packed full of pensioners, sitting round tables, playing cards. Where they all came from, and how they got there, remained a mystery. The place fell silent as they took in the apparitions that had appeared in the doorway, in full lycra, and covered in sweat and road dirt. We might as well have landed from an alien space craft. This was not the kind of place to try to order a cappuccino, but they did manage a reasonable Caesar salad – heavy on chicken and with tons of what passes for cheese in Montana. Folk there were very friendly, and wanted to know all about the ride. We spent a happy hour refuelling, explaining the shirts, and absorbing the community atmosphere. Roll on retirement.

Thompson Falls was the only place big enough to have accommodation in the entire valley, and we were forced to accept a relatively low mileage day. We checked in early at the cheap motel right next to the falls. Compared to Kettle Falls, these had fared a little better at the hands of the hydro engineers, but not much. The river was dammed in concrete, just a few hundred metres upstream from the falls. In high summer, the trickle escaping over the lichen-encrusted cliffs was pathetic, with almost the entire river passing through the subterranean turbines. The main point of interest was a fish ladder, added quite recently to bring salmon back to the upper river. It was a crazy, avant-garde construction - a spiral of steel grating and plastic tubing, part water slide, and part exhibit from the Tate Modern. But it seemed to be doing the job, and whiteboards proudly recorded the weekly counts of a wide range of fish making the surreal, upwards journey.

It was a good job we had had a short day, because in Thompson Falls we moved from Pacific Time to Central Mountain Time and lost an hour of our precious, afternoon recovery time. But it was encouraging evidence that we were moving east. That evening we found another excellent steak bar, with an outdoor terrace overlooking the lake. We watched the deer come down to the bank to drink, and a heron fishing in the shallows. But it wasn't all rural tranquillity. Every half an hour or so, a multi-tone air horn and clanging bell would shatter the peace, announcing the passage of another freight train. The railroad track was only feet from the restaurant, on the other side of the road, and the whole terrace rocked and swayed as the ground heaved under the wheels of the giant train, as it creaked and clanked its way past.

Yes, of course we had to count the wagons. The longest had 200 of them, sandwiched between two power units at the front, two at the back, and another four in the middle. They only travel slowly, and our steaks and beer vibrated their way across the table for fully five to ten minutes, before normal eating and conversation could resume. Imagine our delight when our new friends, Alan and Julie, explained that the trains run all night long. They were a lovely couple and, as the IPA flowed, they got thoroughly carried away and offered us the free use of a spare log cabin for the night, just out of town, away from the trains. Sadly, we weren't up to moving all our kit in the dark, so we spent a disturbed night, dreaming of being mown down by trains, logging trucks, and giant locusts.

A room-only motel meant breakfast from the 24-hour gas station next door. For the first time in the trip, it was cloudy, not just smoky, and rain threatened as we sat outside, next to the pumps, in the grey dawn light, munching sandwiches prepared some time the previous century. Refuelling motorists were aware of our intrusion onto their turf, but they had no protocol for dealing with us. Most had never seen a cyclist before, and just ignored us. More appeared confused, unable to believe that a bike is a viable means of transport over Montana mileages, never mind across the continent. A few were hostile, but that was rare.

The miles that followed were very much enlivened by the passage of trains, often close beside the road. That morning they were all travelling the same way as us, and only slightly faster. The drivers were friendly and would wave, but it proved difficult to count the wagons because, as the trains slowed, we'd start to overtake again, and we'd have to 'uncount' wagons. It seems I have yet to master subtraction. Suffice to say that the trains were very long, and that we were alongside them for ages. Just when we were beginning to tire of this, Alan and Julie pulled up alongside us in their pick-up truck. With the window wound down, they were quite happy to carry on a 20 mph conversation where we'd left off the night before, as though this was the most normal thing in the world. Maybe the guy has a second job as a road race cycle team manager, but he didn't mention it. Anyway, he proved capable of driving in a predictable, straight line, but no bottles or magic spanners were provided.

We rode for 65 miles, up the canyon-like, Clark Fork river valley, whilst gaining less than 100 feet in height. It's so flat that the river just sits there quietly, sulking. This is not the place for a rafting trip. The valley was gouged out by the explosive, Missoula floods, rather than by gradual downcutting. The enormous volumes of high speed water had also carved out the rocky valley sides, and we cycled under huge crags. Side valleys played havoc with the wind direction. One minute we had a good tail wind, and were purring along at 25 mph, whilst chatting to people in cars, just like the pros, and the next minute, the wind was in our faces, and we were struggling, like amateurs, to do 15 mph.

In the late morning, we entered Paradise. Sadly, not a euphoric state of pedalling bliss, but a collection of ramshackle huts and rusting, agricultural machinery, strung out along the road. What must those early settlers have been through, if they thought this was paradise?

At the Bison café, we were on the Flathead reservation, and all the staff and customers were Native Americans. This was another cultural shift from yesterday's white, working class, card sharpers at Trout Creek. The shirts proved, yet again, to be a useful ice-breaker, and the matriarch in charge was prepared to act as dialect coach.

"A Huckleberry Tall Stack with 2 eggs over easy, please" was eventually understood, even in my American accent.

The Bison café is on the edge of the National Bison Reserve. I would have loved to see these animals in their grassland wilderness but, reluctantly, I had to admit that this is one attraction where road bikes are thoroughly impractical. Visitors in pickups, and RVs, drive for miles down dirt tracks from an already remote visitor centre, over steeply rolling hills, looking for the beasties. And anyway, by now it was raining hard, so the bison were probably hiding. Dragging ourselves away, fuelled by eggs and pancakes, we flew up and over a low pass, in heavy rain and equally heavy traffic, and down to Missoula. After 8 days of riding we had completed 689 miles, and we deserved a day off the bikes.

Missoula was a great place for a day off. It's a vibrant, youthful town, with a University campus and lots going on. There was a marathon taking place, with a huge field of at least a thousand runners, of all shapes and sizes. Our hotel was packed full of them, and everyone assumed that we were running too. Not being the heroic centre of attention was a new experience for us, and it took some adjusting to. The weather was back to full heat again, so the marathon started at dawn, to give the runners a chance. We rolled out of bed in time to cheer the late finishers across the line.

From the University campus, there were magnificent views of the surrounding hills. These had hemmed in the ice age, Lake Missoula, and the grassy slopes bore the unmistakeable, horizontal lines of ancient lake shores, stacked one upon another. These shorelines had puzzled geologists for years, before the whole story was eventually worked out. Most impressive was the fact that the lines began about 500 feet up the hillside above our heads, topping out at twice that height, as the lake level had gone up and down over the centuries. I found it mind boggling.

Missoula is the home of the Adventure Cycle Association, where there is a museum celebrating the first transcontinental bicycle trips. But today was Sunday, and it was closed. Our journey was not completely wasted however, because, outside their headquarters, we came across the most improbable bike lane markings I have ever seen. This was a wide, main road in the centre of town, with three lanes for traffic in each direction, and no central reservation. In the middle of the two centre lanes were large, white, bike symbols, painted on the road. Now, admittedly, there have been times when I have complained about bikes not being given any priority on the roads, but promoting us to the completely unprotected fast lane of three was not really what I had been looking for. I'm not sure if our friends at the ACA use these lanes on their way to work but, if so, I suspect that their staff turnover is quite high.

The lack of accommodation between Missoula and Helena meant that we had little choice but to tackle the 128-mile section in one day. It looked challenging, with the first 110 miles being uphill, and with the MacDonald pass lying in wait for us, right at the end of the day. At least it would serve to bring our daily average of just 86 miles, closer to the magic 100, having started conservatively because of all the mountain passes in Washington State. And what a wonderful day's riding it proved to be.

Montana has the kind of stunning, wild west, scenery

that I had only seen in films. Wide open grasslands led to mountains with scattered pines, small derelict wooden barns, cattle in some places, horse ranches in others. There were narrow, wooded canyons with cliffs, through which the road wound upwards to the next open vista. There was hardly any traffic, only one gas station, and two tiny hamlets in 128 miles. Above all, there was always that big, wide open, Montana sky. Wow!

To begin with it was overcast and cool, great for cycling, and we cruised along, drinking in the views. After 50 miles, we stopped at the first sign of life, the Stray Bullet Café, in the tiny hamlet of Ovando. In the 1880s, this quirky old café was a western saloon bar, and a notice tells how:

> 'Bar room brawls erupted, pistols were drawn and fired. Sometimes the cowboy might take a graze in the shoulder, or if he were lucky, the shooter would miss his target completely and have a 'stray bullet'. One of those stray bullets remains immortalized right here in the café wall'.

And there it was, though rather less impressive than the story it had inspired.

The café's evocative website advertised the fact that it had been in the same family for five generations, and three generations of women were on hand to provide us with our second breakfast, and a packed lunch for the remaining 78, almost uninhabited miles. I had been looking forward to this café stop since finding the website, over two years previously, and it didn't disappoint.

After Ovando, the sun came out and we picked up a tail wind. We were still pedalling uphill, but at a good speed. The scenery was as stunning as ever. Huge, tree-dotted, glacial moraines, hundreds of feet high and miles long, swept down from the mountains, and cut across the grasslands.

At the second hamlet of the day, Avon, we had run out of water. The village shop wasn't open, so Tim knocked on a door where we had seen boys playing outside. In these circumstances, I have had varying receptions over the years, but this was one of the best. We were welcomed in warmly, and the lads insisted on amusing us with magic tricks, whilst water and cakes were fetched. You never know what's coming next on a trip like this.

Finally, there was the small matter of the McDonald Pass. I was not used to starting the main climb of the day with over 100 miles in the legs, but needs must. Still, it had been the fastest 100 miles that I had ever ridden, so something was going right. The pass was steep, but relatively short, topping out at 6325 feet, our highest point so far. More importantly, it was the Continental Divide. The old jokes are the best, so I had to have a pee exactly on the top, just to see if it would end up in the Atlantic, via the Missouri and Mississippi, or in the Pacific, via the Colombia River. Unfortunately, I was distracted by a 'Continental Divide Mountain Bike Trail' signboard, pointing up a dirt track (now there's an idea!), and most of it ended up in my shoe. Coincidentally, the shoe was also heading for the Atlantic, but not just yet. We were looking for 4000 miles of scenic heaven, and in two days' time we planned to re-cross the Great Divide, heading back west, before looping round Yellowstone Park and crossing it eastwards for a third and final time. Celebrating the crossing of the Great Divide was thus put on hold for later, and we flew down the only descent of the day, to Helena.

Helena is the sprawling, state capital of Montana, and it has precisely none of the charm of Missoula. In fact, after several miles spent navigating featureless, out-of-town shopping malls, decaying residential suburbs, and urban road spaghetti, we were seriously considering turning around and going back. Our hotel, on the far edge of town, was another bland concrete block, surrounded by fast food outlets. It was too far to go back to the centre of town for our evening meal, so one of these would have to do. In our innocence, we were shocked to discover that these 'restaurants' were really casinos, with a side-line in unappetising carbohydrates. We explained to the doorman at the first, that gambling on fixed odds machines was guaranteed to lose money, over time, and we weren't that stupid. We just wanted food. Strangely enough, we were shown the door. At the second, we managed to acquire tacos, without incident, but they were foul. Luckily, there was a nearby supermarket, where we bought a DIY evening meal to take back to the hotel. Not the ideal nutrition to end a long day in the saddle.

The best thing about being on the far edge of Helena was that we could escape rapidly in the morning. The road was hot, and heavy with traffic, even with an early start. We were cutting across rolling ground, heading south, for the headwaters of the infant Missouri. Almost all the roads we had ridden up to this point had had large shoulders, for the snowploughs to pile the winter snow. For us, these shoulders were a safe, albeit debris-strewn, place to ride. But this time, the shoulder disappeared. The road was narrow, and a high-speed truck in each direction, plus cyclists in single file, were not guaranteed to fit. At home, we would have ridden side by side, forcing vehicles to wait behind us for a safe overtaking space. But here, we had no confidence that truck drivers would even notice us before they rear-ended us, since the concept of cyclists on the road was so alien. The alternative was a tiny strip of tarmac, about 6 inches wide, just beyond the rumble strip. This was an exciting place to cycle. I had ridden in Romania, with Helen, my wife, in just this situation, and I still have nightmares of hearing wagons behind us crossing the rumble strip, onto our precious strip of tarmac, to avoid oncoming vehicles in the middle of the road. In America, the trucks stayed on the correct side of the rumble strip, but their wing mirrors passed over the tops of our cycle helmets at regular intervals. One false move and we were either in the ditch, or under a truck.

The Missouri river rises in the hills just to the south of Townsend, a dusty, derelict, township that didn't have a café, nor anywhere to shelter from the intense heat. Two friendly security guards outside the gas station started chatting. They told us we were crazy. A woman motorist overheard and insisted on shaking our hands, though from admiration or sympathy, who knows? The Missouri is the longest river in the USA, travelling 2341 miles before it joins the Mississippi, which itself travels 2321 miles to the Caribbean. As we crossed the infant river, it was heading for a huge loop to the north, whereas we were heading for a similarly huge loop to the south, around Yellowstone Park. We were not expecting to see it again for another 15 days. We took photos on the bridge, and went our separate ways.

Roadworks loomed ahead, for seven miles, according to the signboard. Brand new asphalt was being laid, and the traffic was making do with one-way, alternate working along a single lane of the old road. A pony-tailed woman in a high viz jacket, brandishing a 'Stop/Go' sign, flagged us to a halt. She was straight on the radio, presumably asking if anyone knew what these bizarre, two-wheeled, pedalling machines were. Not suitable for riding through with the traffic, was the verdict. Fair enough really, because the lane was far too narrow. After some debate, we were told to enter the 'live' roadworks, and to ride the slick, new asphalt, that was quietly steaming in the heat. Obediently, we slalomed between the cones, and hit the black stuff. I soon realised that I was lacking some important information. What is the temperature of asphalt as it's laid down? How fast does it cool, when the air temperature is 100F? What is the rate of heat transfer between hot asphalt and a rotating bicycle tyre? And, most important, what is the melting temperature of a bike tyre? I tried asking Tim, but he only has one response to any difficulty:

"Just keep pedalling!"

"Faster, or slower?" I asked. "Which will heat the tyres more?"

But Tim was gone. Then the real fun started. A huge team was blitzing the roadworks at high speed. There were trucks delivering the hot asphalt, machines spreading it, and steamrollers compacting it ready for the next layer. There must have been 30 or 40 vehicles, hard at work, over a couple of miles, and we had to weave the best line through the middle of the organised chaos. Trying not to be buried in asphalt and steamrollered, stopped me worrying about the tyres.

We emerged unscathed at the far end, but the bikes were in a mess. The frames were spattered with lumps of hot, sticky tar, and the tyres were caked in it. This time I was confident that I knew the relevant piece of information.

"Light oil is an excellent solvent for heavy oil" I announced, triumphantly.

This was a discovery I had made as a youth, by unexpectedly cleaning my black, oily fingers after working on my bike by the simple expedient of using them to eat fish and chips. And providence had blessed us with a ready supply of lightly-oiled, fast food wrappers, conveniently discarded by passing drivers. These were perfectly sized, wet-wipes for bikes, and they made short work of the job.

The wrappers may have been useful, but 24 hours on fast food was taking its toll. My legs felt empty, for the first time on the ride. Perhaps they were responding to the emptiness all around us. We were high up, on a broad saddle between low hills, with parched grasslands stretching for miles in each direction. There were no buildings in sight, but every now and then we would come across a gateway of three timbers, like a goal post with a name board on the top, belonging to a cattle ranch. There would be no sign of the ranch itself, mind you, just a dirt track leading to the far-off horizon. This is Big Country, Montana.

So, it was quite a surprise when we suddenly reached Manhattan. Skyscrapers were in short supply, but The Manhattan Garden Café was an oasis of cool, and it served long-overdue, proper food. The moustachioed Swiss owner regaled us with talk of all the long-distance cyclists who had passed through his café. He was the first person so far to take our journey in his stride, as a perfectly normal activity, and I didn't know whether to be pleased or not. We were not alone in our madness, after all.

Belgrade, where we spent the night, was only a short hop from Manhattan. As we left town, the next morning, we knew we had another massive day ahead. In 122 miles of cycling, we were planning to climb up the Gallatin river valley, to gain access to the high plateau next to Yellowstone Park. The first 70 miles were all steadily uphill, following the river. Rain threatened as we set off, and the high country ahead was hidden under thick cloud. The valley was deeply incised, with cliffs jutting from the forested slopes, and the valley floor was lined with open meadows, where horses grazed beside the magnificent river. The river wound ferociously from side to side, which made for constantly changing vistas. The only settlement in the valley was at Big Sky, at the base of a ski station. Here we ate the biggest second breakfast so far, in a restaurant full of holidaymakers, the first we had seen for a while.

The going became tough, as a headwind began to increase, in tandem with the gradient. Tim was disappearing ahead, and I was starting to suffer. White crosses beside the road, often in groups of 4 or 5, marked a shocking total of 38 road deaths in the Gallatin valley, and didn't help my morale. It seemed unlikely that any of these had been from exhaustion, and I wondered if I was about to start a new trend. And yet there were encouraging signs of progress. As we climbed, the trees began to thin out, the river shrank slowly to a stream, and the meadows were suddenly alpine. When the summit arrived, at last, it was only a flattening in the road, with very little descent ahead. We sat silently at the top and ate the remainder of our food, for the first time a little daunted by the scale of our undertaking.

But we were up on the plateau, and when we reached West Yellowstone, after 100 miles of cycling, we were very close to the Park's west entrance. The town was heaving with tourists, and I had no energy to hunt for a suitable place to eat. We ended up in a dingy cabin, with surly staff to match. There was cherry pie on the table in front of me, though I was too far gone to be able to eat it. Here it was that Temptation visited us, in the guise of a Short Cut. After all, you can't spend 40 days being tested in the wilderness without it. The Temptation was to give up on the remaining 22 miles for the day, and to find a hotel in West Yellowstone for the night. Then we could enter the Park the next day via the West Entrance, reaching Grant's Lodge by Yellowstone Lake in an easy day's ride. But this was the Broad Road that leads to Hell. Whereas the planned Narrow Road to Heaven took an extra day to reach Grant's Lodge, first crossing the Targhee Pass and skirting south down the west flank of the Park, then crossing the Teton Pass, and entering the Park via the South Entrance. I really wanted to stick to the planned route, to see the Teton Mountains, and to explore more of Yellowstone. But I was knackered, and the temptation was too much for me. Reluctantly, I pulled my phone out and began to search for accommodation in West Yellowstone.

Somewhere, my guardian angel stirred into life. Miraculously, there wasn't a bed to be found anywhere in town, despite my best efforts. We had no choice but to carry on along the Narrow Road, towards the Targhee Pass. Yet, as we did so, it didn't feel much like Salvation. More like Judgement Day. As we approached the pass, thunder rolled, and lightening flickered from the south. The high ground of Yellowstone Park disappeared under an inky, black veil. On the slopes of the Targhee Pass, the edge of the approaching storm hit us hard, with huge, icy hail stones driven straight into our faces by a strong, gusty wind that was surprisingly cold. At the top, we were on the Continental Divide again, but this time heading back towards the west, and re-entering Idaho. We were also at 7072 feet, a new height record for the trip. The hail on the leading edge of the storm was giving way to freezing cold, torrential rain, and I was done in. I knew that, in these conditions, the additional 15 miles or so to our hotel would take me forever, and the effort would be difficult to recover from in time to ride again the following day.

Straight away, I convinced myself that my next idea wasn't really a Temptation. At worst, it would be a minor Lapse. Tim was digging out his rain jacket, his bike leaning on the Targhee Pass summit sign board, his back turned towards me and the road. Seconds later, my thumb was out, asking for a lift, and almost immediately a pickup pulled in to the layby beside me. Giving Tim no time to protest, I threw my bike into the flat back of the truck and climbed in beside the driver. Tim had little choice but to follow suit.

Inside the cabin of Mike's pickup, all was order and tranquility. The carpet was thick, the furnishings tasteful, there was Country and Western on the radio, and Mike sat in his shirt sleeves in air-conditioned comfort, without a care in the world. Meanwhile, outside the vehicle, it had turned as black as night, a wall of water was hurling itself against the windscreen and roof, and soon we were driving through lakes of deep, standing water.

I consoled myself with two thoughts. First, we could

afford to lose the remaining 15 miles of cycling, because the planned route was about 4070 miles. We would still complete 4000 miles. Even better, the miles in Mike's pickup were taking us mostly south, but also back to the west a little. So not cycling them wasn't cheating at all, it was more like common sense. I settled back to enjoy the ride.

Mike was planning a cycle ride of his own the following day, and he had been reconnoitering the conditions up in Yellowstone. Mike was very keen to make us understand that the Park's weather can be dangerous, even in summer. He had driven up there to check the river levels, and the snow conditions. He had been happy to rescue fellow cyclists, partly, it seemed, because our plight validated his cautious approach. The good news was that there was little snow remaining in the Park, the forecast predicted a period of settled weather to follow the storm, and Mike was good to go the next morning. Very kindly, he made a detour of several miles to drop us off at the Angler's Lodge, beside the Henry's Fork river.

I am not a fisherman, and I am no fan of blood sports, but the Angler's Lodge was one of the best hotels of the trip. This magnificent log building stands in glorious isolation, right on the bank of this beautiful, wild river. Picture windows give views of the river, and the forest beyond. The walls are covered with moose heads and stuffed animals, mostly fish. For us, this was very upmarket - our first hotel with a restaurant. Unfortunately, I was so far gone that I had to lie down for several hours to recover before I could cope with eating anything, reviving only just before the chef clocked off for the night.

4 YELLOWSTONE PARK AND THE BEAR TOOTH HIGHWAY

In the morning, a mist hung low over the river. Over breakfast, we watched as the sun began to come through, and the mist broke into patches that slowly evaporated into nothing. This was magical, and quite the best way to start a day. I would very much like to return to Angler's Lodge, perhaps for a proper holiday that doesn't involve thousands of miles of cycling.

Back on the bikes, we found that there was a welcome chill in the air, commensurate with the altitude. We turned onto the Mesa Falls Scenic Highway, a quiet back road for a change. We were crossing the edge of the Henry Fork Caldera, an underground magma chamber, second only in size, and potential destructive force, to the one sitting underneath Yellowstone Park itself. It's a good idea to tread lightly in these parts.

The pine woods of the Scenic Highway soon gave way to rolling, Idaho farmland of barley and potatoes. In the distance, away to our left, we could see the line of the Grand Teton mountains, lightly capped with cloud. Even at this range, they were a magnificent sight. Just as well, because this whole, unnecessary, loop to the south was mainly so we could appreciate them from all angles. We were about to almost circumnavigate them, all except their northern flank. Tim began to dream of a return for a mountaineering trip. We spent the rest of the day closing in on the Tetons, and then riding south, down their western flank. By now it was very hot indeed, and the southerly wind was against us. Hard going, once again, but my legs seemed to be working surprisingly well.

The final task for the day was to cross east, over the mountains, via the Teton Pass. Somehow, I kept designing routes where the big climb came right at the end of the day. This one was a real brute. The approach was plastered with sign boards warning of 'Severe Gradients Ahead'. There was also a weight limit, and a weigh station for trucks. There was no one around, so we pulled in, to discover that the equipment was fully functional. I cycled on to the weighing road, and obtained a readout of 181 lbs, (81 kg). That's me, the bike, my luggage for two months, and two bottles of water. Not bad. For the record, Tim was 222 lbs, (100 kg), and he claimed that the extra was all muscle.

It still felt far too heavy, as we hit the steepest slopes towards the top. The gradient climbed above 10%, and stayed there for what seemed like forever.

"You must really want to see those *******
mountains", was Tim's pithy comment on my stupid route design, as we toiled upwards, one pedal stroke at a time.

Tim rarely complains, and swears even less frequently, so that tells you how crazy this whole idea was. RVs crawled past us, with their engines screaming. I loved it, of course. The steeper the better at my weight. But all good things must come to an end and, eventually, the summit overlook car park came into view. Here a motorist leapt out of his car and high-fived us enthusiastically.

"My car was struggling to get up there", he said, "Never mind you guys!"

He photographed us, under a sign reading 'Howdy Stranger. Yonder is Jackson Hole, the last of the Old West'. It was worth the photograph, because this was another new height record at 8430 feet, and we had entered Wyoming, our fourth state.

The dead straight descent was every bit as steep as the ascent, and here it was that Tim finally broke through the 50 mph barrier. Sadly, I failed to grab his wheel as we left the summit, and could only manage an exhilarating 48

mph. We were still enjoying the buzz, when a car pulled up alongside us, the window came down, and a middle-aged woman started shouting at us.

"You guys are idiots. You could have been killed, back there".

She should have seen us lying in the road, photographing logging trucks on the Wauconda Pass. Some people just have no sense of what's dangerous and what isn't. The trouble is, I'm not sure whether that's her, or us.

Sitting just south of Yellowstone Park, Jackson, Wyoming, is a tourist town that dines out on its wild west credentials. The central square has an enormous pile of moose antlers at each corner. It was a relief to find that these are collected after being shed, naturally, and we were not about to find a mound of decaying moose carcasses to match. The town had an Asian restaurant that served excellent stir fry chicken and vegetables with noodles, quite the tastiest meal of the trip so far. For the first time, we saw tourists by the coachload, many of them Chinese, but one full of Amish people, in traditional Amish dress. That night, I had a sense of a corner turned, literally and metaphorically. Now, at the furthest point in the loop, we were turning back north and then east. The forecast was set fair for several days, and the continuing southerly wind would be on our backs. We had ridden over a thousand miles, I had survived a crisis in the storm on the Targhee Pass, and the three days ahead were surely going to be the Crown Jewels of the entire route.

And so it proved. The days spent cycling north from Jackson, through Yellowstone National Park, were the most spectacular of the entire ride. It was a complete sensory overload. A smorgasbord of mountains, lakes, rivers, waterfalls, canyons, bears, bison, eagles, geysers, hot springs; everywhere you looked there was another jaw dropping natural wonder. And all this was in perfect weather, and with a light wind on our tail. It was like being in heaven. For once, the imperative to keep moving was almost entirely balanced by the desire to linger along the way and to drink it all in.

We had been warned about the dangers of cycling through Yellowstone. Not the stampeding bison or the marauding grizzly bears, but the distracted drivers of huge, hired, RVs, with no idea how wide they are. But we were pleasantly surprised. First the general speed of traffic was much lower than usual, and the holiday drivers were very patient and courteous. Second, there were no heavy trucks. Only the most essential of supplies are allowed in: Kentucky Fried Chicken, McDonalds, Starbucks, Ben and Jerries' Ice Cream vans, Coca Cola tankers, and so on. But I'm not complaining. The visitor centres, usually in the most interesting places were mostly a welcome upgrade from our usual, ugly, gas stations. Some had interesting exhibitions, and all had friendly staff to mind our bikes.

At the start, there was even a proper, useable, bike path. Going north from Jackson, a segregated bike route snaked its way through the sage grass prairie, up and over a low pass, to reveal the true majesty of the Tetons, seen from the east, towering above the Snake River valley. There was snow high up on the jagged peaks, and wisps of white cloud projected into the blue sky above several thousand feet of near vertical rock. The iconic photo from here has the Teton National Park signboard in the foreground, hanging from a huge frame of Lodgepole Pine trunks. We were in awe. Tim was gracious enough to admit that, despite the swearing, it really had been worth the effort on the Teton Pass.

Still on the bike path, we weaved between the glacial moraines on the valley floor to Jenny Lake, nestling in a hidden fold at the very foot of the mountains. This is one of those secret places, full of magical peace and serenity which, in the Himalayas, would probably be considered a sacred 'beyul'. Even here, in the most visited park in the USA, with parking lot, visitor centre and restaurant, Jenny Lake still has an aura about it that draws you in. It was early in the morning and, with few people about, we cycled the well-made footpath to the lakeshore and simply sat, and stared. And then sat and stared some more. We took some photos. And then we sat some more.

Maybe it was because we had entered some higher dimension, or perhaps it was just the tailwind, but we floated on along the Teton Park Road beside Jackson Lake in a state of transcendental bliss. I hardly noticed that we had stopped for coffee in an overpriced, motorway service station style cafeteria; because the central mall at Jackson Lake Lodge has the biggest and the best picture window I have ever seen, anywhere. Fully 60 feet tall, this window framed an elevated view over the lake to the Tetons beyond that had to be seen to be believed.

Now on the John D Rockefeller Jr Parkway, we joined the main traffic heading for the Park's south entrance. The sight of the iconic, log cabin toll booths, took me straight back to Yogi Bear cartoons I had seen as a kid, and to Yogi's attempted escapes from Jellystone Park. Our brush with Yogi's 'Ranger Smith' was very friendly indeed. Once again, our shirts were great at explaining the trip at a glance, and Mr Ranger, sir, waived the entrance fee, but very unofficially. I'll carry on calling him Ranger Smith, despite his name badge, in case of repercussions. In fact, I spent the next few miles wondering whether we would have to show a ticket to be let out of the Park at the other end. If so, then I would be raiding the memory banks for Yogi Bear's Jellystone Park escape techniques.

A climb up beside the Lewis River Canyon, deep in beautiful, Lodgepole Pine forest, brought us to Lewis Falls. Here there was evidence of the major wildfires of 1988, with areas of the forest only just regenerating, almost thirty years later. The falls themselves were another great place to stop, and we sat munching cakes and admiring yet another great view. Our agreed rule for the whole ride was that whenever one of us wanted to stop, for absolutely any reason, then the other stopped too, and no complaining. This meant that we pretty much doubled the number of stops that either of us might have made individually, particularly for photos, and that was fine. But I do not recommend Yellowstone for a large group ride, at least not using our stops rule. You would never get anywhere, since someone would be able to find a reason to stop every few yards.

We met two Scots guys who were doing the same as us; cycling across the USA, from west to east. Strangely, we were riding the same road in opposite directions at the time. They had taken the sensible route through Yellowstone, west entrance to east exit, but they were riding touring bikes piled high with camping kit. I can't say that they were in the best of spirits, what with the slow pace, and all the weight they were carrying, and a full two months' hard labour still ahead of them. When they found out that we were looping round, adding miles just to pull in some extra sights, and still aiming to complete in 40 days, it was close to the final straw. I almost had my bike stolen by one of them, under the pretence of lifting it to assess its lightness.

Lewis Falls led on to Lewis Lake, which was the final body of Pacific-bound water that we would see. Shortly afterwards, we crossed the Continental Divide for the third and final time. We had to queue for the obligatory photos under the signboard, before finishing early for the day at Grants Lodge, beside Yellowstone Lake, still nearly 8000 feet above sea level. Grants is the oldest of the visitor lodges in the Park, and we had enough energy left to walk along the lake shore, enjoying the remoteness of the terrain, and the wildlife. We saw mule deer, chipmunks, red squirrels, white pelicans, and trumpeter swans.

But if you have any imagination at all, Grants Lodge

isn't the most soothing place to stay. Here, the West Thumb of Yellowstone Lake is the circular result of the most recent super volcano eruption, about 174,000 years ago. This eruption was extremely explosive, because of the instantaneous release of dissolved gases, and all the overlying land fell into the empty magma chamber of the caldera, forming the circular depression. And this was only a small one, relative to the series of such super eruptions over the past two million years or so. In that time, the North American tectonic plate has been moving in a south westerly direction, whilst the underlying hotspot has remained stationary, so that the site of the caldera eruptions appear to be moving north eastwards. The current bulge of the magma chamber over the hotspot, known as the Sour Creek resurgent dome, was the line of low hills that we could see across Yellowstone Lake to the north east. The Sour Creek eruption is overdue, of course by geological time periods, but the bulge was growing at an above-average 3 inches a year between 2000 and 2008 in response to growing magma pressure. But all is well; the latest thinking is that the magma chamber does not contain enough gas for a full scale, explosive super eruption, just a bog standard one, though I can't claim to have slept soundly that night.

The build-up of tourist traffic in the previous afternoon, and the knowledge that we would want to stop frequently, encouraged us to make a very early start the next morning. We were rewarded with an ethereal mist, drifting low over Yellowstone Lake in the calm, cold air. We quickly realised that this was coming from the hot springs of the West Thumb Geyser Basin. Stopping within a mile of the start was a new, short hop record, but these were our first geysers, and they were unmissable. Raised, wooden boardwalks allow visitors to peer through the plumes of steam into the circular, hot pools. With no one else around, we could treat the elevated boardwalks as a bike park, which added to the entertainment as we sought out the best pictures.

At the end of Yellowstone Lake, we took one final look at the weather forecast for the following day, and turned north. This was a moment of commitment, because the Beartooth Highway reaches 10,947 feet and is exposed for many miles to violent, summer storms. Snowbound for nine months of the year, it is only opened at the very end of May. Even in mid-summer, storms can easily bring snow and very high winds. We had already had a small taste of this on the Targhee Pass. But with the sun shining, and the early morning chill gradually giving way to the promise of another very hot day, it was hard to believe that there would be any problems ahead.

We followed the Yellowstone River, downstream from the outfall of the lake. Geysers lined the road: some full of hot water, others full of acid. The valley itself was almost impossibly beautiful. Only a few weeks from the height of the snow melt, the river was still powerful, sometimes dropping rapidly over small cataracts, sometimes winding its way more slowly across alpine meadows. Except that they couldn't have been alpine, because these meadows were studded with bison, and you don't see those in the Alps. Round the next bend, several vehicles had stopped, partially blocking the road. People were out of their cars, cameras in hand, because a group of bison were walking steadily downhill, quite close by, and heading directly for them. At Grants Lodge, we had been told an unlikely sounding story about a tourist posing for a selfie with a bison behind them. The poser had been gored in the back, or so the story goes, and the Rangers had been warning people to stay away from bison. By the time the magnificent beasts arrived, everyone else had climbed safely back into their vehicles, and we had an uninterrupted, heart-stoppingly close view. The huge animals weaved their way across the road between the stationary cars, studiously ignoring us, and headed for new pastures beside the river. Over the following miles, we became quite blasé about cycling past roadside bison, often stopping to coax them into posing for our cameras, but we refrained from bison selfies.

Our next animal encounter was even better. A crowd of perhaps a hundred people were lining the road, binoculars and telephoto lenses pointed towards the river, at this point about a quarter of a mile away. And there, unmistakeable even at that distance, was the distinctive outline of a huge grizzly bear, and her cub, fishing in the shallows. A Park Ranger confirmed that it was unusual for the grizzlies to venture so far towards the road as to be visible to tourists. But we weren't complaining. A friendly family lent us some binoculars, and we lingered for ages, watching the bears pulling salmon from an idyllic, braided section of the river. Sadly, the photos are disappointing because of the distance, but I'm not sure that I'd have wanted to be much closer. Not on my bike, anyway.

From this point, the river began to pick up speed, heading purposefully for the Upper Falls, and then its spectacular plunge over the Lower Falls into the Grand Canyon of Yellowstone. We climbed up and away from the river to ride the North Canyon Rim Road, and to visit its series of lookout points. An osprey passed overhead as we arrived at the first viewpoint, demonstrating the immense scale of the scenery by disappearing as a speck in the distance long before it reached the end of the canyon, and the 300-foot-high, Lower Falls. This is an impressive height for a big river to fall in one clean, uninterrupted, drop, and the canyon walls reverberated with the thunder.

Unable to follow the river down the canyon, the Grand Loop Road is forced to take an alternative route over the Dunraven Pass, on the flanks of Mount Washburn. This was a beautiful, gently graded climb that took us to alpine meadows just above the tree line, and long-distance views south over the Park. At 8859 feet, it was also the latest height record for the trip. An extra reward was a long, exhilaratingly fast descent, with excellent sight lines. We overtook a whole series of cars and RVs on the bends as we flew, headlong, down nearly 3000 feet of mountain. At Tower Falls, where the road re-joins the Yellowstone River valley, we stopped for lunch at a fast food outlet, the only bad one we found in the Park. We sat outside, marvelling at trays piled high with tacos, chips, burgers, ice cream, and one litre cartons of sugary drinks. By some miracle, we had managed to find a chicken salad (albeit the high carbohydrate version, with lashings of an unidentified sauce, potato mayonnaise, and plastic cheese) but were still only eating about half the average quantity of carbohydrate and sugar that most people were putting away for lunch, despite our 6000 calories a day exercise regime. Not surprising that even the ten-year-olds weighed twice as much as us, and could only just waddle from car to burger bar and back.

We crossed the Yellowstone River, heading for the little-used, north-east Park entrance. On a short, steep descent I hit a pothole at high speed, and punctured my front tyre. We pulled off the road at a convenient spot, where a Ranger's vehicle was already parked. The young woman Ranger was preparing a family with two girls for a back country, guided walk. As I fixed the puncture we listened to the advice on 'What to do if we meet a bear'.

"Back away slowly, and don't run", the Ranger said.
Tim noticed the kids looking increasingly anxious, and so did the Ranger.

"But we probably won't see any bears today", she said quickly. Unfortunately, I was not quite on the same wavelength. Full of enthusiasm, I piped up,

"You might see one. We've just seen two grizzlies, relatively close, only a couple of hours ago. They were fishing in the river".

The Ranger drew herself up to her full height, bristling

hostility. We backed away slowly.

Bears are not the only danger hereabouts. The Lamar valley is home to one of Yellowstone's most studied wolf packs, and a long stretch of the road was marked with regular signboards warning people not to get out of their cars. There were no instructions for cyclists, however, so we could only follow Tim's regular rule, applicable in any difficulty – 'Just keep pedalling'. In this section, we had our final encounter with bison, when a cow and three large calves came galloping across a road bridge, at high speed, in the opposite direction to us. The traffic came to a halt, and I took shelter behind the fender of the car in front, while Tim stood in the road and shot video of them thundering past. Sadly, we didn't see any wolves.

The broad valley began to narrow, and fork, with the road taking the narrowest, and least likely looking of the available options. We lost the grasslands of the wide valley floor, and began to climb more steeply through woods, between cliffs on both sides. On reaching the Park exit, we escaped without having to show a ticket, and carried on climbing, to reach Cooke City. This seems an odd place, geographically, for a settlement, given that it is far too high up the Lamar valley to have any cultivatable land. We had climbed back up to 8000 feet again. But it was, of course, a gold rush town from the 1870s, now trading on its wild west past and reliant on tourism. I really liked the tiny little place, and a superb steak was a fitting finish to one of the best days of the trip.

Our high-altitude day dawned bright and clear. With no expectation of food or shelter for 70 hard miles, we raided the rather meagre breakfast buffet mercilessly, so apologies to the hotel's late risers, and we left with our pockets bulging with bananas and blueberry muffins. The Beartooth Highway is a very special road. Built in just four years, and opened in 1936 under legislation designed to promote road access to National Parks, it passes right over the top of a beautiful mountain range that I can only describe as being like the Cairngorms on speed. Switchbacks lead up though Larchpole Pine forest to an exposed summit plateau, with alpine, semi-tundra moorland, very like that in Scotland, only at 11,000 feet, rather than 4000. As in the Cairngorms, dramatic cliffs define the summit plateau, sheltering lochans in corries. But here the cliffs are much taller. From the summit, the Beartooth Highway descends 4000 feet, pinned to the vertical walls of the Rock Creek Canyon, on a 6% grade over 7.5 miles. It is an engineering triumph, recently re-engineered after being partly washed away in 2005. No wonder that it is one of only 10 Scenic Byways to be awarded the highest accolade of 'All-American Road'. I had spent the previous two years looking forward to riding it, avidly following the progress of the snow clearance each May, with spectacular photos and video posted online by the Montana Department of Transport.

To reach the start of the main climbing, we had to cross the Colter Pass and descend the Clark Fork River valley for about 10 miles. In the early morning air, this was a chilly business, but the road was deserted, and we had great views of the distinctive rock fang of Beartooth Mountain itself. Tim put it on his mountaineering 'to do' list, which was filling up nicely during this trip. With the chilly descent completed, I was anxious to get warmed up and, with 4000 feet of climbing spread over 20 miles, there was plenty of opportunity for that. I am never happier than when at the bottom of one of these monster climbs, with three hours of pure heaven to look forward to, and this was no exception. After the first banana, we had reached the top of the lower forest and were nearing a line of huge crags. A blueberry muffin later, and we had wound up through a narrow canyon in the cliffs to the upper mountain, above the tree line, and the Beartooth Lake, nestled idyllically under its own crag. The unexpected appearance of the 'Top of the World Store', conveniently at the half way point, saved our dwindling food supplies because, although it mainly sold tourist tat, it also had a small café. We became quite the centre of attention amongst the families and the groups of passing motorcyclists alike. Most people seemed to think that they had achieved something significant, even adventurous, in driving their vehicles to 9000 feet above sea level, and they couldn't quite grasp that we had cycled up, fuelled by bananas and blueberry muffins. This isn't like the Alps, where cyclists are commonplace.

From the café, the second half was a series of gigantic switchbacks, past high altitude glacial lakes, across the barren tundra, winding up through crags towards the summit plateau. Magnificent. Tim and I were deeply into our own rhythms and thoughts, and quite a gap opened between us. Passing drivers and motorcyclists shouted encouragement as we pedalled onwards. More bananas and blueberry muffins were converted effortlessly into upwards motion until, all too soon, it was all over, and I had reached the top of the road. Tim was already there, and he had recruited an enthusiastic family to photograph us both under the signboard. The kids posed with us, enjoying the vicarious thrill of our achievement.

When we'd had enough of questions, we moved away from the crowds and found a sunny spot, out of the wind, to finish off our supply of muffins. The views to the north were sensational. In the foreground, and just below us, was a section of semi-tundra, snowfields, and crags, cut across by a huge canyon whose bottom we could not see. Beyond the canyon, a jumble of rocky mountain peaks and glaciers disappeared into the distance. There was no sign of humanity whatsoever. At 10,947 feet, (3337 meters) this was, by far, the highest I had ever been on a bike. There is no surfaced road this high in the Alps. In fact, there aren't many places in the world where you can go higher on tarmac.

It was just 12 noon, and it had taken us four hours to cover the 30 miles from our Cooke City hotel to the summit. We still had another 70 miles to go but, luckily, it was all downhill. Literally. 7,600 feet of uninterrupted downhill, to be exact. This is a descent record that I am unlikely to break any time soon. The biggest dilemma, while dropping into the canyon, was whether to hurtle down, concentrating on the adrenaline rush, or to take it steady, with regular stops to drink in the awesome scenery. We settled on the latter, stopping where the road runs along the canyon rim, and then at all the overlooks on the way down. We had the advantage of being able to stop on narrow, twisting sections of road, where cars had to keep moving, and so we could hang out over the crash barriers in the wildest sections. At times, it was hard to believe that the ribbon of tarmac that we could see, stacked in layers, far below, was the same road.

When we reached Red Lodge, we were starving, and we demolished an enormous late lunch in a busy café, full of motorcyclists. This was a dirty, humdrum sort of a town, full of traffic and noise. Or perhaps it was just the contrast with where we had been. Because, as we ate, the elation of the past three days slowly gave way to feelings of regret that we were leaving the beauty of Yellowstone behind. Anyway, we decided that it was time to stop meandering around, time to get our heads down, and to put in some big miles, due east across the plains. In this sort of mood, and with a huge energy rush from the food, we tore on down the valley road, riding hard as a pair, taking egg-timered turns on the front for the first time for ages. A long section of gravel through some roadworks, and then a puncture, slowed us down a bit, but even so we knocked out the 70 miles from the summit to Laurel in not much over two and a half hours. It really had been a day of two halves - one up and one down.

5 MONTANA REVISITED

Laurel is on the Yellowstone River, which had taken a big loop round to the northwest since we'd left it, the previous day. In Laurel, its banks are studded not with bison, but with chemical works. It is hemmed in by freeway and railroad track, not by forest and mountain. The contrast was enormous, and quite saddening. Nothing but fast food outlets surrounded our out-of-town motel so, lacking the energy to forage further afield, we found ourselves back in Pizza Hut. It would have been easy to have become depressed, so it was time to look ahead, to the next challenge.

Our next target was the Black Hills of South Dakota, over 300 miles away across some very remote grassland. This huge area is home to the Crow and to the Northern Cheyenne tribes, and we would be riding across both reservations. For us, the problem was the absence of well-spaced motels, meaning that we would have one short day, and then two long days of well over 100 miles each. At least the short, first day would give us a chance to find a bike shop in Billings, and allow us to take it easy. However, the forecast still promised afternoon temperatures above 100F, and we decided to make an early

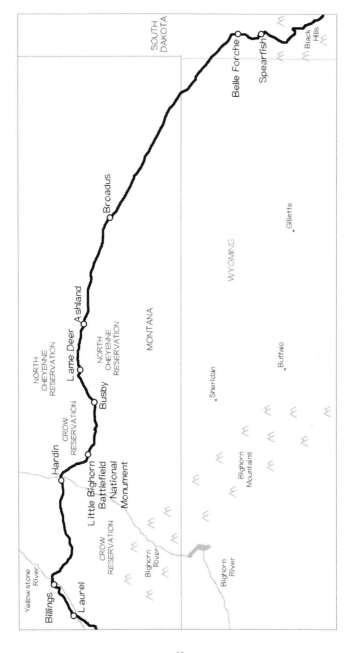

start and at least reach Billings in the cool of early morning.

So, when Sarah and Jason arrived for work at The Spoke Shop, they were surprised to find us, sunning ourselves on the grass outside their shop, waiting for them to open. Thankfully, they were generous enough to shelve whatever they had been planning to do first thing that morning, to sort us out and to service our bikes. Both had plenty of long distance rides under their belt, including some huge challenge rides over the Beartooth Highway, so they knew it well. The shop was an oasis of calm, and we drank coffee and chatted, whilst the mechanics gave the bikes a quick tune up. Talk turned to close encounters with wild animals in Yellowstone, and elsewhere. Sarah and Jason warned us that rattlesnakes were quite common in the area, and that they have a habit of sunning themselves on the red-hot concrete of the shoulder, right where we usually ride. This was not a pleasant thought. We replenished our dwindling supply of inner tubes, and they wouldn't take anything except a contribution to the beer fund. Bike shops have a very special approach to capitalism, and I love it. This was a very laid-back start to the day.

Speaking of capitalism, Billings is the largest city in Montana, and it has all the wealth and vitality of a rapidly expanding oil town, thanks to the nearby Bakken oil field. The Bakken field has been at the centre of a long battle over the building of the Dakota Access Pipeline, running southeast across four states, to refineries in Illinois. When we passed through, in the summer of 2015, there was a growing movement of Native Americans and environmentalists, trying to block its completion. This led to a legal challenge by the Standing Rock Sioux, who lost in Sept 2016, only for President Obama to step in and call for a moratorium. That moratorium still holds as I write this at the end of 2016. Crude oil is still moving by railroad, but the planned development of the field has been severely restricted. This will not last much longer. President Elect Trump owns a significant stake in the pipeline project, and the main oil company was a major campaign donor.

On leaving the bike shop, we headed straight into Billings city centre. We soon found ourselves amongst posh hotels and high-end clothes shops, which was not ideal when we only wanted sun cream and some food. We paused outside a café, where a group of older men were having coffee in the sunshine, trying to figure out where to go to find a local convenience store. One of them, Bill, was also a cyclist, and he wanted to know all about the ride. On hearing that we were looking for sun cream, Bill walked to his car and produced some to give to us, along with directions to the supermarket. It seems that Billings is full of kind people.

They are inquisitive too. Whilst buying our lunch in the supermarket, everyone wanted to talk about the ride, intrigued by the slogans on our shirts. One of them, a young woman in a suit, explained that she worked for the Billings Gazette. Before we knew it, she had produced a camera and interviewed us for the paper. Under the headline, 'British bicyclists trying to complete 4,000 miles in 40 days', she wrote, 'In Billings, Ralph and Hill attracted plenty of attention as they stopped outside the Albertsons on 27th Street, stocking up on water and cookies for the ride'. Fame at last.

We needed the water, because the temperature was soaring again, and we were heading out into the sparsely populated grasslands of the Crow Reservation. This was a different landscape from any we'd seen before, much drier than western Montana. Following Old Highway 87, to avoid the Interstate, we climbed up through some low hills to a superb viewpoint. Rolling, sandy coloured grasslands, stretched to each horizon, with no sign of human life except for a remote farmstead on a distant hill. However, we were under surveillance. Groups of unbroken horses eyed us suspiciously from a distance, snorting noisily. Marmots kept popping their heads from their burrows, hundreds of them it seemed, with the bolder ones playing above ground before bolting back down the nearest hole. They were great to watch, but very difficult to photograph. The only interruption to the grasslands was a series of dry ravines that cut through the hills. With their low cliffs, and winding courses, these canyons were classic 'ambush' country, and scenes from wild west films kept playing, unbidden, through our heads.

By lunchtime, we had reached our destination, the small town of Hardin. We had no choice but to stop, because the next accommodation was 120 miles further down the road. We were very glad of the aircon in the motel, and did not venture outside until an evening thunderstorm lowered the temperature a little.

Hardin's only claim to fame is that it is the nearest town to the site of the Battle of Little Bighorn, famous for Custer's Last Stand. Since 1881, five years after the battle, there has been a National Cemetery and a Memorial for the 268 dead of the 7th Cavalry Regiment. This was the Custer Battlefield National Monument, with no mention of any Native Americans. Astonishingly, it was not until 2003 that Congress approved the addition of an Indian Memorial, and a change of name to the Little Bighorn Battlefield National Monument. Ironically, not only were the victorious Lakota and Cheyenne warriors edited out of the story, they also lost their nomadic way of life in the aftermath of the battle, and they became confined to reservations.

Long distance cyclists can be very shallow individuals, and the battle site did not hold our attention for long. Apart from the cemetery and the two monuments, the site looks much the same as all the surrounding grassland.

Crucially, the site has a Deep Ravine, that allowed unobserved movement, but it looked just the same as all the ravines we had seen the previous day. We were more concerned about the fact that the site did not have a café. Having had a very poor motel breakfast in Hardin, we were relying on finding a full scale second breakfast. Some rapid internet research suggested that this would be available at the nearby gas station. The website said that the Crow tribe ran this gas station and café, and having previously visited the excellent one run by the Flathead people, near Missoula, our hopes were high. Sadly, we arrived to find the whole site boarded up, out of business and closed. A couple of aggressive-looking, underfed dogs snarled at us, but that was it. As with so much in divided America, people offered competing explanations. In Broadus that night, the white people told us that it was because Native Americans are incapable of running an effective business. That's the polite version. In Lame Deer, the Native Americans told us that local white people had boycotted it because of its ownership. Either way, we cycled the rest of the morning on empty stomachs, with low water supplies, and only a handful of fig rolls.

But we didn't have much to complain about, given the living conditions of the Cheyenne people that we saw as we sped through the reservation on our expensive steeds. Busby, with a population of 747, was made of dilapidated porta cabins and looked like a shanty town. The 2000 census says that 39% of the population of Busby is below the US poverty line, which is up there with some of the most deprived inner-city districts. The village of Lame Deer, in the middle of the reservation, was even more of a shock. First, there were loads of people on foot, walking up and down the sides of the broken-up roads. Several were staggering about, clearly off their heads. A few beaten-up station wagons were the only cars we saw, and wild horses seemed to have priority on the roads. Packs of dogs scavenged menacingly. None of the rundown buildings were labelled, so it was hard to tell which, if any, were shops. The gas station toilets were blocked and filthy. I had seen nothing like this, except perhaps in Africa. Most people ignored us, but the staff in the hot deli that was attached to the gas station were friendly enough. The thermometer read 103F as we sat outside amidst the chaos, guzzling litres of cold water, and slowly refuelling.

Culturally, this was a million miles away from the tourist hotspots of Yellowstone Park. It was another America altogether. Yet the scenery throughout the reservation was stunning. I had not expected to enjoy such a harsh, semi-arid landscape, but it was beautiful. Stands of Lodgepole Pine studded the rolling hills, and circular sandstone towers of various colours from yellow to red stood out from the grass.

Without warning, Tim slammed on his brakes and skidded to a halt, forcing me to do the same. There, on the shoulder of the road, right in front of us, was a large rattlesnake, with its conspicuous tail. It was a good job Sarah and Jason, in Billings, had warned us to be on the lookout, and that Tim has fast reactions. This rattlesnake, however, was not moving. We plucked up the courage for a slightly closer inspection, and still it didn't move. But how lively would you expect a rattlesnake to be in the searing midday heat? Perhaps it was taking an after-dinner nap. We realised first, that we didn't know anything about the post-prandial habits of rattlesnakes and, second, that we were in danger of venturing into Monty Python 'Dead Parrot' territory. If it had indeed kicked the bucket, shuffled off 'is mortal coil, run down the curtain and joined the bleedin' choir invisible, if it had become an ex-rattlesnake, then there was no sign of damage to its body, so it probably hadn't been run over. Perhaps it was just resting. There was only one way to be sure, so Tim summoned his inner 7-year-old and poked it with a stick. Luckily for him, it was indeed an ex-rattlesnake. Its cause of death is still unknown, but perhaps its supply of passing cyclists was not frequent enough to keep body and soul together.

We were cutting across the drainage, and the road rolled constantly up and down. In Ashland, whilst refuelling on cold drinks at a gas station, we met the local Sheriff, who wanted to know about the ride. As with so many people we met, the real amazement came when he found out that we were not using a support vehicle, and we were entirely self-reliant. He seemed seriously concerned about us when he realised that we were heading back out into the 110F heat for the remaining 45, remote and uninhabited miles to Broadus. I think he was about to prevent us from leaving, but Tim managed to distract him by getting a camera out. The Sheriff was very happy to be photographed, in his cool shades, hand on holstered gun, standing beside his huge 'Rosebud County Sheriff' pick up. Later, we wondered whether his presence in Ashland had anything to do with a huge, cylindrical, pressure tank that we met travelling, very slowly, in the opposite direction, on the back of a massive, 48 wheeled, low-loader. It was clearly something to do with the oil industry, and several security vehicles were escorting it.

On the very edge of Ashland, we found the self-proclaimed, 'Best Little Bordello in Montana'. This had been recently renovated in wild west style, with veranda, and horse-hitching rail outside. With another couple of hours of hard cycling ahead, we rode on without testing the veracity of the claim, but it looked convincing enough. The remainder of the day was tough, but thoroughly enjoyable, and by the end we had ridden over 120 miles, with 5000 feet of ascent. We collapsed into a tiny motel in Broadus, the only one for miles around, and turned the aircon up to maximum.

Broadus was a very strange place indeed. It had a tiny

shop, where a group of old men were playing cards in what appeared to be a scene from 'League of Gentlemen'. The proprietor bristled with suspicion and hostility as we walked in. Not being local was clearly a serious crime. Worse, by having the names of faraway places on our shirts, we risked giving the game away to his inmates. I could just imagine one of the card players getting up and accusing the owner, "You lied to me, Edward! There is a Swansea!" (Or perhaps, Seattle). Adding to the weirdness was the fact that the boarded-up cinema, right opposite the shop, had a child's doll, bound by the waist, lashed to each of the wooden uprights along its veranda. These macabre bodies dangled there, looking for all the world like the corpses of gagged and bound children. No explanation was offered. Quite bizarre.

The only place to eat in Broadus was the Powder River Stockman's Club. It looked like a dodgy private club - a windowless, wooden cabin, set back from the road - but we were assured we could get a steak. A lone waitress sat behind the bar, wearing cowgirl boots, a skin-tight, white dress, and not a lot else. We sat right underneath the front end of an enormous cow, projecting from the wall. It stared across the room at its compatriots, similarly stuffed, mounted, and adorning all the other walls. To add insult to injury, the whole herd had to watch us eating the biggest and most fabulous steaks we had yet encountered. They were unlike any steak I had ever had before. The texture was that of a ripe cheese, and the whole thing just melted in the mouth. The flavour was stunning, and the full 16 ounces went down in seconds. Wow!

Breakfast the next morning, however, left a lot to be desired. A yogurt and a bagel were all we could find in the tiny, self-service, motel kitchen. We were back on the road, hungry again, around 6.30 am to beat the heat. As we left town, a convoy of massive bull-nosed trucks hauling double trailers with huge John Deere combine harvesters passed us in the opposite direction, heading west. There must have been 20 of them. It seemed a bit strange, since we hadn't seen anything except prairie grass for the previous 200 miles, but I guess that the convoy was travelling long distance. Agriculture is done on a vast scale around here.

This was a second, 120-mile day, and the first time we had tried to string two long days together, back to back. Trees were becoming fewer and farther between, as were the settlements, and we had nothing but the endless, rolling road for company as we piled on the miles across the parched grasslands. But, as the sun grew hotter, the wind began to get up, and before long it was blowing hard.

The Great Plains of the USA are, of course, renowned for their winds, and there are plenty of horror stories told by misguided, east to west, transcontinental cyclists. Mostly, these involve gnashing of teeth, and crying in roadside ditches. My close study of the climate data for August on the Great Plains showed that for four days out of five the wind blows from the west or south-west, and the rest of the time, strangely, in almost exactly the opposite direction. There are hardly any calm days, and average afternoon wind speeds are around 25-30 mph. This four to one ration explains why we were cycling west to east. And it also meant that I had been prepared to put back-to-back days of up to 150 miles on the forthcoming schedule across the Great Plains. These long days would balance out the shorter mileage days across the mountains at the start of the ride, and take the average back towards 100 miles a day. But the strategy was a gamble. A succession of days with easterly winds, and we might well be crying in ditches ourselves.

So, it was reassuring to pick up a strong westerly as soon as we started onto the plains, just when we needed it. Soon we were floating along effortlessly, with the miles flying past under the wheels. In such open country, the road was usually visible down long straights, far into the distance. In other conditions this might have been daunting, but we soon became used to the idea that in five or ten minutes' time we would be on the distant horizon, and the next expanse of empty grass, with a ribbon of road, would have opened before us. Who needs a car?

By mid-morning, we reached Alzada, the only sign of human habitation in the 95 miles from Broadus to Belle Forche. There were just two buildings; a gas station and the derelict looking, Stoneville Saloon. This was a wild west style saloon bar, with a sign promising 'Good Beer, Lousy Food' and 'Topless Tuesdays'. An odd day to choose, we thought. It being Thursday, we hitched our bikes to the sun-bleached timbers of the hitching rail and engaged in the rather more wholesome pursuit of posing for photos on a collection of outlandish, Mad-Max inspired, tricycles, made from old beer barrels and beaten up wheels.

You can tell we were feeling pleased with ourselves, because all this messing about took precedence over the serious business of finding a breakfast in the gas station. It was a good job that pancakes, eggs, bacon, and maple syrup were all available in the usual vast quantities, because the first breakfast had been so poor, and we were seriously hungry again.

Soon after Alzada, we left Montana for the final time and re-entered Wyoming. In fact, it only took a few minutes to cut diagonally across Wyoming's top right-hand corner, and then we were in South Dakota, our fifth state. Having to stop twice in such a short space of time to photograph state boundary signs was a bit annoying when we'd been making such fantastic, uninterrupted progress. At the South Dakota State Line, we chatted with a family with young children, who had stopped to take the same souvenir photo. It was the ninth state of their holiday and, like us, they were heading for the Black Hills of South Dakota. But, sensibly, they had only been visiting each state once, and they were puzzled by our rather circuitous route, and the fact that we had visited Montana, Idaho, and Wyoming twice each. But we knew that this wandering about could not continue if we were to reach Boston in just another 23 days of riding and, from now on, we planned to visit new states only once each.

By now, we could see the Black Hills in the distance. They towered over a broad plain, onto which we were gradually descending, at speed, powered by the wind behind us. On the edge of the plain was Belle Forche, the largest town since Billings. Its outskirts were a culture shock, after nearly 300 miles of grass. There were acres of farm machinery laid out in fields for sale. There were garages with row upon row of giant four by fours. There were sheds full of fencing, warehouses with barrels of weed killer and pesticides.

We decided to head into the centre of the old town to try to find a decent café for lunch, rather than make do with one of the huge gas stations on the outskirts. But the small, historic centre was completely hollowed out, with boarded up wooden buildings, and most of the remaining shops closed. The entire commerce of the place had migrated to the malls on the perimeter, and the centre seemed to have folded entirely.

A couple of miles later, in the usual characterless desert of shopping malls, gas stations, and fast food outlets, we were surprised to find what we'd been looking for in town. Patty's Place was a high quality, family run, wholefood restaurant, with an excellent chicken salad, and friendly staff. Thank you, Patty! Ninety-five miles covered, and it was only just after 12 noon, so we were on a bit of a high. And so was the temperature. The digital display at the mall entrance read 94F (34C).

After lunch, the landscape changed dramatically. As we approached Spearfish and the Black Hills, we turned off onto a quiet backroad which ran between arable fields, with hedges and fences. These small fields were well irrigated with small streams, and were very green. There were some expensive houses, with horses and paddocks.

But just as I was starting to think that I might be in Kent, I spotted a bright blue bird perching on a fence post beside the road ahead, quite unlike anything found in England. As we approached, it took off and began to fly along the road right beside us, keeping pace only a few feet from our heads. Suddenly it was like being in one of those wildlife films, where a camera drone gives a close-up view of a bird in flight. It was a striking creature, about the size of a starling, but bright blue all over, and it seemed just as interested in us as we were in it. It stayed with us for a couple of minutes, before peeling off and heading towards a nearby copse of trees. Subsequent investigation leads me to think that it was a Mountain Bluebird.

Spearfish was our first tourist destination since we had left Yellowstone Park three days earlier. It is the northern gateway to the Black Hills, a dramatic outcrop of granite, rising out of the plains to an average height of around 6000 feet. But most noticeable straight away was the large number of motorcycles parked in front of our motel. A thunderstorm coincided with our arrival, and we were pinned down for an hour or so by torrential rain, along with the motorcyclists, to whom we got talking. It emerged that they were preparing to attend the Sturgis Rally, a venerable American institution that we knew nothing about. It turns out that Pappy Hoel's old Motorcycle Classic has been held in Sturgis, a town about 20 miles east of Spearfish, every year since 1940, making this the 75th edition. As the advertising says:

'For people who love motorcycles, Sturgis is a mecca - a destination sought by pilgrims - and once August rolls around the truth of that becomes clear. They come like some fantastic form of weather, like lightning rolling down the Interstate, bringing a unique chorus of thunder. They rumble in alone, in pairs, or in packs, weary from the miles but excited to arrive, and they ride up Legendary Main Street to park and stretch their legs and take it all in'.

But the most dramatic part of it, for us, were the huge numbers involved. By the end of the 1970's, attendance was averaging 30,000, then it exploded in the 80's, to more than 300,000 by the time of Pappy's death in 1989. By the year 2000, the attendance had reached 633,000. For the 75th rally they were expecting anything from 750,000 to a million motorcyclists. Locals could earn a small fortune by leaving the area and renting out their properties for the duration. The good news for us was that the opening of the rally was still two weeks away, and we would be well to the east by the time the advance guard we had met was fully reinforced.

After the thunderstorm, we walked into the centre of town, only to find Main Street, through which we had ridden only a couple of hours before, completely sealed off. The four lanes of roadway were gridlocked with classic cars, maybe about 100 of them, mainly from the 1950s and 1960s. I don't have any great interest in classic cars, but I must say that some of these were things of great beauty, and the pride of their owners was well justified. The heavy rain had caused some consternation, and there was much mopping and polishing of paint and chrome. They didn't seem to realise that water drops on polished surfaces made for some interesting, arty photographs, and we wandered round for some time.

Dinner that evening was in the Bay Tree Café. The original wooden building was erected in 1892, as the Queen City Hotel, and it has that classic, stepped, wooden façade above the shop front – a façade that shouts, 'Wild west'. A recent restoration means that one of the oldest surviving wooden buildings in South Dakota is now a thriving community hub, serving great food. Indeed, we had to queue for a table, it was so busy. The local speciality is Walleye, the state fish, and a kind of pike. It made a very acceptable change from steak.

6 THE BLACK HILLS

Having ridden just under 250 miles in the previous two days, we planned to take things a little more slowly in the Black Hills. There is such a lot to see and, although we couldn't possibly do it all justice, nonetheless we wanted enough time to see some of the highlights. And as it turned out, the day from Spearfish was one of the best days of the whole trip. The first of the highlights was the Spearfish Canyon, where our road wound upwards beside the Spearfish river, between cliffs of oolitic limestone a thousand feet tall. These rose straight out of dense woodland, the beautiful honey colour of Cotswold stone shining strongly in the early morning sunshine. The contrast between this majestic canyon and the open prairie of the past few days could not have been more dramatic. The climb was at an easy gradient, but unrelenting, so we were happy for the excuse to stop and photograph Bridal Falls, where a small river comes straight over the cliff edge.

Two thousand feet higher up, at the head of the canyon, at Cheyenne Crossing, we found a café for a second massive breakfast, only just over an hour since our first. There were some families on holiday, but the clientele was mainly motorcyclists, ahead of the Sturgis Rally. The sinuous curves of the canyon road were an obvious attraction to motorcyclists but, surprisingly perhaps, there was none of the thrill seeking, speed obsessed motorcycling that blights the Yorkshire Dales in the summer months. These guys were content to amble along, admiring the scenery, and generally driving in a thoroughly responsible fashion. It turned out that this was entirely typical of the friendly and respectful motorcycling that we

were to witness over the next couple of weeks.

Soon we were pedalling up steeper gradients, heading back to 6000 feet above sea level. Somebody had been painting cycling slogans on the road. But these weren't the names of cycling stars, such as on alpine climbs in Europe. They were altogether more gnomic. The first said,

'Decided now if you are going to get to the top?'

Followed by,

'Yes?' and then 'YES!'

After a mile or so,

'Burn legs, burn'.

After another mile,

'Know what you are thinking'.

And then, finally,

'Where is the ***** top?'

Well the top came, eventually, but there was no sign of any valedictory slogan. It was altogether a strange series of messages, but it amused us, and took our minds off the pain in our legs.

We had now gained access to the upland expanse of beautiful, rolling alpine forest and meadows that make up the Black Hills. This land holds many sites that are sacred to Native America peoples, but the early settlers and the US government couldn't see much use for it, since the harsh climate and dense forest at this altitude means it is not an obvious place for cultivation. So, in 1868, during a brief period when the Lakota held the upper hand in the ongoing skirmishes with the settlers, the US government ceded the Black Hills and its hunting rights to the Lakota, in perpetuity, closing it to settlers. But the Treaty of Laramie, as it was known, lasted just six years. In 1874, General Custer's expedition led to the discovery of gold in the Black Hills, and an instant gold rush saw miners pouring into the area. In 1877, the US government formally reneged on the Treaty of Laramie, took back the Black Hills, and forcibly reassigned the Lakota to smaller reservations down on the plains. There is, however, a 20th century codicil to the story. In 1980, the Supreme Court ruled that, in 1877, the government had taken the land back illegally. The Court awarded the Lakota Sioux $15.5 million for the market value of the land in 1877, along with 103 years' worth of interest at 5 percent - that's an additional $105 million. But the Lakota have refused to accept the money, continuing with their claim to the land itself. Partly this is because the land is clearly far more valuable than this, and that the money would not go far if split among 100,000 Lakota people. But it's also because of the fundamental principle of refusing to cede sacred lands for money. The compensation money is currently sitting in a Bureau of Indian Affairs bank account, earning compound interest.

We contemplated this legal impasse as we turned onto the North Rochford Road, heading south towards the centre of the Black Hills. This fabulous road rolled up and down through forests of Ponderosa Pine and Black Hills Spruce, from time to time opening out into small valleys, with areas of cultivation and attractive farmsteads, followed by more forest, with small lakes and granite crags. There was no traffic, and only the sound of birdsong from the woods. This was my kind of cycling.

But we were in danger of creating an impasse of our own, because we knew that the tarmac road ended after 15 miles or so, at the tiny hamlet of Rochford. Beyond that point there are only rough gravel tracks, quite impassable on our lightweight, narrow wheeled carbon fibre road bikes. Our plan was to follow the Mickelson Trail, a converted rail line, for about 20 miles, through the heart of the Black Hills, to Hill City. But even this trail was not tarmacked. The trail website describes the surface as 'mainly crushed limestone', with the warning, 'thin tire road bikes: not recommended'.

As it happened, our first taste of off-road riding came about sooner than expected. Approaching Rochford, we were stopped by a woman in a hard hat and orange overalls, brandishing an oversized stop/go lollipop. This was the usual, low tech, traffic control for the roadworks ahead. These women must have mighty trades union representation. Or perhaps they have not yet invented mobile traffic lights in the USA. Anyway, as usual, she was straight on the radio.

"I've got two cyclists heading south".

We couldn't hear the reply.

"Two cyclists", she repeated.

There was another pause. Clearly this wasn't making any sense.

"Guys on pedal bikes".

But once identified, there appeared to be no protocol for dealing with cyclists. After some discussion, they threatened to send a lorry to ferry us through. This might have been welcome on some previous roadworks, on major roads with heavy traffic, narrow lanes between the cones, and hundreds of busy roadworkers in the live section. But this was a tiny, virtually traffic free road in the middle of nowhere. There's a time and a place for being Health and Safety conscious. The idea was ridiculous, and we refused. A standoff ensued. Eventually, after some persuasion, it was agreed that we could proceed, at our own risk. The surface had been removed, leaving loose dirt and chippings, but the only real danger was a solitary steamroller about half way down the hill to Rochford.

The Moonshine Gulch Saloon in Rochford was a real gem. The exterior is classic wild west saloon: square wooden building with veranda and hitching posts, and the name across the top in big letters. But it's the interior that really stands out. Every nook and cranny of the walls and ceilings is covered with memorabilia of all kinds, mostly left by previous visitors: business cards, baseball hats, t-shirts, $1 bills - all with people's names written on them. Add in the usual trophy deer heads (antlers adorned with tin hats, of course), bon mot slogans, and musical instruments for that spontaneous jam session, and you have a unique, Aladdin's cave of oddities of all kinds, including a working jukebox from the 1950s. The young guy behind the bar was suitably taciturn, with a very dry sense of humour. We found ourselves regretting that we wouldn't be settling in for an evening of local beer, steak, and craic.

Instead, we prepared to join the Mickelson Trail, and set off into the wilds, away from any roads and settlements. But Americans really do like their wilds to be properly tamed. They are very Health and Safety conscious in Rochford, as we had already found out. First, we had to make sure that we were aware of all the possible trail hazards. According to the information board, these included:

- Starvation (bring food – it's 20 miles to the next refreshment)
- Dehydration (bring water - see above)
- Sunstroke (wear a hat - take plenty of rests)
- Exhaustion (some of the railway gradients reach a challenging 4%)
- Accident or emergency (no phone coverage – always travel in groups, minimum of three)
- Mountain lions (DO NOT RUN)
- Rattlesnakes (RUN)
- Poison ivy (DO NOT TOUCH)

We hadn't realised that cycling in the countryside was such a dangerous business. In addition, we discovered that access to the trail was by pre-purchased permit only, and that numbers were rationed in the summer months, with on-the-spot fines for transgressors. We figured that it was a bit late to tell us that, after we'd already committed to 20 miles of otherwise dead-end road to reach the trailhead. Anyway, reading that long list of instructions had put us in the mood for breaking rules, so on we went, without permits.

Straight away, we were transported to another world. In our imaginations, we were riding a classic American steam locomotive, with oversized, funnel-shaped smokestack and cattle-catcher on the front. We rolled along beside a beautiful mountain stream, with herons wading, and buzzards overhead, until the line crossed over, high above the water, on one of those long, wooden trestle bridges that I had only ever seen in films. This first one had at least seven layers of trestles and must have been nearly a hundred feet above the river. We stopped and climbed down the sides for photographs. Several more followed in quick succession. On one of them we met Shari, all the way from Chicago, and Cindy, from New Hampshire, cycling mountain bikes. They were on a short holiday ride, out and back along the trail. Having read our shirts, they wanted to know all about our ride, and they seemed awestruck by the distances involved.

"You guys must be so fit!"

Well, I can't speak for Tim, but I must admit that I am not used to being the subject of such undisguised female adulation. Indeed, we had been without female conversation of any kind for some time and, somehow, the chat just seemed to keep going, and going. The drive to keep the pedals turning seemed mysteriously to have deserted us. After some considerable time, I noticed adulation beginning to mutate into concern – I think they were wondering if this was developing into a hostage-taking situation – so, reluctantly, we let them go on their way.

The river had now entered a winding, narrow canyon between cliffs. We saw plenty of deer in the woods on either side of the track, and a skunk. Then we reached our first tunnel, where the entrance was an iconic shape that stopped us in our tracks. Instead of the horseshoe cross section, that we were used to seeing in the UK, usually in brick or concrete, this was almost square. It consisted of three gigantic wooden beams, with the two side timbers leaning inwards slightly, and topped off by a huge, horizontal crossbeam. Once again, we had only ever seen this kind of construction in wild west films, and we were enchanted. The inside of the tunnel was supported in the same way throughout, and we puffed through, doing our best steam whistle noises.

The breath-taking scenery just kept going, on and on. The trail emerged from the narrowest part of the gorge and began to climb into more open ground. Here, the long grasses of the wild meadows were turned purple with wild bergamot, growing in profusion under the scattered pine trees. This landscape appeared to be entirely untouched by humanity.

The only fly in the ointment was the quality of the surface we were riding on. It was well-compacted, and relatively smooth, but there were some rough patches, and plenty of holes and scattered rocks to watch out for. Our long-suffering backsides were not impressed, and soon began to let us know. Progress was slow and painful, in stark contrast to yesterday's high-speed dash across the plains. (Was that only yesterday?) The high spirits of the first hour on the trail began to ebb away, and we pedalled on, mainly in silence.

"I shall be glad to get back to tarmac", I ventured, after a while.

"I'm glad you said that", Tim responded, "The trail's been fantastic, but I've had enough now".

We stopped for a break at some old station buildings, where a hand pump had been fitted to a well head. This was fun, and it was good to have some upper body exercise, for a change. Whilst drinking the strangely delicious, crystal-clear, mountain water, we spotted a gravel road about half a mile away, across virgin meadowland. The map indicated that the gravel road led, in a short distance, to a tarmac road, saving us several miles of the rough Mickelson Trail. The temptation was too much, and we decided that it was time to try off-roading in style – never mind rough tracks, we were going to plough right across the intervening, uncultivated meadow. I am pleased to report that we managed it without resorting to walking, though it was touch and go, and a considerable amount of the meadow grass had to be removed from the drive trains afterwards. But at least it's a nicer job than removing road tar, or mangled locusts. Half an hour later we rolled into Hill City, after a very slow, but thoroughly memorable day, of only just over 60 miles.

Hill City is a gold rush town, par excellence. It sprang up in 1876, almost overnight and, although the miners soon switched to tin, not gold, Hill City developed a formidable reputation for gambling, drinking, and prostitution. The classic description was, 'a town with a church at each end, and a mile of Hell in between.' There were said to be no less than fifteen saloons on Main Street.

These days, the churches are still there at each end of Main Street, but the mile in between is full of tourist souvenir shops and fast food outlets. The temptation is to do a joke about it still being a mile of Hell, but that would be unfair on the place. We really enjoyed our afternoon of relaxing and sightseeing in Hill City. Timber buildings dating from the early 1900s line the main street, now containing shops with names redolent of the wild west; such as Buffalo Bob's (Bill's great grandson?), The Broken Arrow Trading Company, and Desperados. Large scale public art was the order of the day: life sized horses made from assorted pieces of scrap metal; chain saw art, featuring bears and mountain lions, some big enough to ride on; weather vanes; well heads; windmills for water pumps. There were two interesting museums, packed with information about the history, and natural history, of the Black Hills. Main Street was busy with holidaymakers, but not crowded, and there was a real buzz about the place. As a calm and peaceful dusk settled, we sat on a veranda after our steaks, drinking a very good glass of local IPA and watching the world go by. Live music was playing from the bar across the road. Embedded as we were, in the very heart of our ride, with so much, already, to remember, and so much to look forward to - life seemed very good indeed.

The second of our short days of sightseeing in the Black Hills was to feature the Mount Rushmore National Monument, where the faces of George Washington, Thomas Jefferson, Theodore Roosevelt, and Abraham Lincoln are carved out of the granite. It had been a choice between this and the Crazy Horse Memorial. The latter is being built to celebrate Crazy Horse, the warrior who led the Lakota to victory over General Custer at the Battle of Little Bighorn, and was treacherously killed by a US solider a year later, having entered Fort Robinson for peace talks, under a flag of truce. It is another vast exercise in granite carving, started in 1948 and still unfinished. Sadly, for us, Mount Rushmore and the Crazy Horse Memorial are in opposite directions from Hill City so, having agreed to stop wandering around in loops, we had to choose between them. Mount Rushmore is in the correct direction and, for that reason only, it got our vote.

The original idea had been to get to Mount Rushmore by circling right around Black Elk Peak which, at 7244 feet, is the highest summit in the Black Hills. But that involved a huge amount of additional climbing, and our legs were sore from the all the hills they had tackled the previous day. So, we cheerfully cut another 15 miles from the route, confident that the total distance remaining was still about 30 miles over the target of 4000 miles. The road across the north flank of Black Elk Peak was stunning, and it gave great, tree-lined views of the granite outcrops that make up the summit. Horse Thief Lake was a little gem. Its mirrored surface held superb reflections of the mountain, towering above lakeside granite crags. It reminded me of Tarn Hows, in the English Lake District.

Over the next few miles the granite outcrops grew steadily taller and more dramatic. We came around a corner to find a huge rock face directly in front of us, and to hear the unmistakeable climbing call of, "I'm safe!" echoing from above. We skidded to a halt and began scanning the cliff. There they were; two tiny figures in the middle of an expanse of nearly vertical granite. As rock climbers ourselves, this was our kind of sightseeing, so we settled down to watch the show. It looked very steep, and the granite was smoothly rippled, like the icing on a Christmas cake, with a complete lack of any obvious crack lines for protection. It looked like a very bold lead. But just then, the leader reached up, and we realised that he was clipping the climbing rope into a bolt, pre-drilled into the route for safety. Being Brits, we had assumed that such a big mountain route would be climbed traditionally, without bolts. But, bolted or not, it was still a great lead, up a stunning piece of rock, leading to an airy pinnacle where the triumphant climber topped out, silhouetted against the bright blue of the sky. We were distinctly jealous.

Back on the bikes, we rounded another long series of curves, and suddenly found ourselves staring at the famous presidential heads of Mount Rushmore. It was then that it dawned on us that the rock face on which we had been watching the climbers was the reverse side of Mount Rushmore itself. I half expected President Roosevelt to be reaching back to scratch the itch on the back of his neck. For some reason they don't allow rock climbing on the Monument side of the mountain, where the heads are, but it looked as though there were some good lines there too. The most promising was probably an HVS, through the beard of president Lincoln and up the left side of his nose.

We were having to make our own entertainment, because the Monument itself was a disappointment. If the tourist shops and museums of Hill City had had a certain amount of wit and charm, then Mount Rushmore seemed to have none. It was far less interesting, and much more predictable. Of course, there was a vast car park and, with nearly three million visitors a year, we could hardly complain about that. But did it have to be placed right in front of the mountain, filling the foreground, and wrecking the view? More surprising to us was the lack of interpretation of the site, considering the huge visitor numbers. A new Visitor Centre had a 20-minute video running on a loop, and not much else, and video clips are best on the internet. It needed a far more imaginative approach; information about the Black Hills, the history, geology, flora, and fauna of the area. Yes, Guzton Borglum's original Sculptor's Studio has recently been restored and is said to house various items of interest, including a 1/12th model of the carvings, but it is tiny, big enough for about 20 people to enter at once. Three million visitors a year is over 8000 a day on average, and probably nearly twice that in the summer when most people visit, let's say 15,000. The Studio is open nine hours a day – so that's less than a minute per person per visit, even if they don't all arrive at once. Let's just say that the queue was enormous, and wasn't going anywhere in a hurry.

As we wandered round rather aimlessly, wondering what to do instead of queueing, understanding began to arrive, albeit slowly. We were approaching this as outsiders, and completely missing the point. Wit and charm was not what people come for. I think it was the Avenue of Flags, the monumental walkway leading up to the Presidents, which first gave the game away. It is clearly laid out as a religious, processional pathway. Americans come here as a form of patriotic pilgrimage, part religious and part nationalistic. Borglum himself is quoted as saying:

"We believe a nation's memorial should, like Washington, Jefferson, Lincoln, and Roosevelt, have a serenity, a nobility, a power that reflects the gods who inspired them and the gods that they have become above".

For Americans, this site is entirely dislocated from its place in the local history, or geography. Or, at least, the connections are mythic rather than real. Above all, this is an emotional experience, one that is religious or quasi-religious depending on your point of view. And the vagueness of the feelings involved is, arguably, part of the power. Clearly the site makes some kind of statement about the 'civilisation' of the west of the country, about the sacredness of the core American values that emerged from the struggles to survive the harshness of frontier life – strength, inventiveness, practicality, individualism, as idealised in the Presidents. But really, like all good pilgrimage sites, what you make of it is up to you. Interpretation is unnecessary, and unwanted. What seems clear is that millions are attracted by the prospect of meditating on, and reinvigorating their faith in their nation.

Having belatedly achieved this insight, we needed refreshment, so we fought our way through the throng in search of the Carver's café. This looked precisely as though three million people a year had been passing through it for at least twenty years. It was like the worst motorway service station you have ever been in. A minute was quite long enough. As foreigners, we also decided to skip the patriotic meditation, so we jumped straight back on our bikes.

The great thing about receiving a revelation on a sacred mountain top is that, from there, the cycling is all downhill. Steeply downhill in this case, so we could terrorise the drivers of RVs once again by overtaking them at close to 50 mph on the switchbacks going down into the town of Keystone. Since I have called these visitors to Mount Rushmore 'pilgrims', I should perhaps say something about their chosen mode of transport, and about the material aspects of nationalistic pilgrimage.

These pilgrims had not taken any vows of poverty, and they certainly hadn't set off on foot, in just the clothes they stood up in. One of the RVs that we overtook on the descent into Keystone was typical of many that we had seen in the Black Hills. The body shell was that of a 50-seater, single decker coach. Living space, including a full-sized lounge, bedroom and bathroom took up the main part of the bus, behind a huge, luxury cab designed for the driver and a single passenger. Yes, the whole bus, 45 feet long, was accommodation for a middle-aged couple on holiday. But these things are difficult to take into town and park, so towing behind was a full sized pick-up truck (not just a tiny car, such as you sometimes see behind a camper van in Europe). On the back of the pick-up truck were two pedal cycles, as though to demonstrate the pilgrim's green credentials. It amused us to think that they were probably away for a similar length of time as us, and covering a similar distance, and yet we were carrying our entire luggage in a tiny bag under the saddle, and we were still overtaking them.

Peaceful backroads took us northeast towards Rapid City, where we were planning a rest day. We badly needed to find a bike shop, since close inspection of Tim's rear tyre revealed that the rubber was worn right through to the canvas in places. Our off-road adventures in the Black Hills had come at a cost, and it was a miracle that there had been no punctures so far. This was a Saturday, so although we planned a rest day in Rapid City on Sunday, the shops would be shut. We needed to push on and get to a bike shop that afternoon. We joined the main, dual-carriage road, Highway 16, just outside Rapid City and found a place for lunch. Once again, the car park was full of motorbikes and, once again, we caused a stir by being the only ones on two wheels not heading for the Sturgis Rally. By now we had noticed that the reaction amongst motorcyclists, whilst generally friendly, was split into two camps. Some were really interested in our ride, and very encouraging. They had usually travelled westwards to get here, and so they wanted to compare routes, and to tell us about places to look out for. Others just shook their heads in disbelief, concluded we were insane, and ignored us.

Rapid City nestles in the lee of the Black Hills, back down on the edge of the plain, at around 3000 feet. The last few miles of our route took us along 'Skyline Drive', a spectacular road along the crest of the final ridge of the Black Hills. We could see the Mount Rushmore away in the distance, and Black Elk Peak beyond. At our feet lay Rapid City, with Rapid Creek curving right round the north end of our ridge, from one side to the other. We stopped at a viewpoint, and got into conversation with a family on holiday.

"You see that big park down there, and all those parking lots, near the creek? Well, that used to be housing, but it was all destroyed in 1972, in the floods. More than 1000 houses were swept away. I lived here, as a kid, and I remember that night. It was pitch black, the power went off, and the water just kept rising. There were wooden houses floating down the creek. 200 people died. It was terrible."

Mike explained that they now lived in Alabama, and they were visiting the Black Hills, his favourite place in the whole USA, on holiday.

"But I just had to come back to Rapid City to see what they've done with the rebuild" he said. "And this is such a good viewpoint, though it's not well known. You did good to find it".

It was clear that the visit was stirring some strong memories, and we stood there in silence for a while, imagining the chaos of that June night, as a wall of water ripped through the valley floor, destroying everything in its path.

On a lighter note, I asked Mike about the Dinosaur Park that was just along Skyline Drive. I had imagined it might have information about local fossil finds, and exhibits.

"Is it worth a visit?"

Mike laughed.

"It's a children's play park, with plastic dinosaurs to clim b on. They did find a dinosaur footprint once, near here, but the nearest major fossil finds are in Wyoming".

Local knowledge had saved us some embarrassment.

We rolled down the final curves at the end of the ridge into Rapid City, where we checked into a huge hotel in the centre of town, and set off to the nearest bike shop. Not only did Tim need a replacement tyre, but his bike had developed an annoying knocking noise, though whether from bottom bracket or front wheel we couldn't quite decide. Dan, at Black Hill Cycles looked at it, and rode it up and down a lot. He found it very difficult to identify the cause of the noise, but suspected grit from the Mickelson Trail. While Dan worked, he and Tim compared notes, and soon established that they had a friend in common, a guy who used to work at Boneshakers – a cycle shop in Harrogate, North Yorkshire. It's a small world.

7 THE BADLANDS

Our day off in Rapid City was an excellent chance to rest, and to take stock. We were half way through the time, having completed 20 days of riding, but we had covered just 1784 of the 4000 miles, at an average of 89.2 miles a day. This meant that in the remaining 20 days, we had to cover 2216 miles at an average of 110.8 miles a day. Rather worryingly, a glance at a small-scale map of the USA shows that Rapid City is only just over a third of the way along a straight line from Seattle to Boston. This is what comes of taking a meandering route. The good news was that we were very much on the planned schedule, we were both fit and well, pedalling strongly, and thoroughly enjoying ourselves. Nonetheless, we both understood that the next five days would make or break the ride. We were planning to ride 616 miles across the Great Plains, through South Dakota and Minnesota, to reach Minneapolis in five days' time.

The obvious conclusion was that food was needed - a lot of it - and preferably washed down with local beer. So, we were delighted to find the Firehouse Brewing Company, the perfect place for it. This elegant, brick and sandstone Rapid City Fire Department building, built in

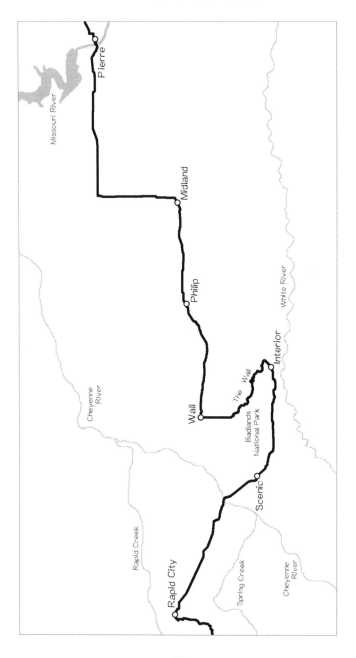

1915 in the Chicago School style, had been recently converted to house a craft brewery, with a bar and restaurant. The first floor used to be accommodation for the fire crews, with the fire trucks downstairs, and the firefighters slid down a smooth brass pole when the fire call came in. The modern bar, sited in the bays housing the fire trucks, is adorned with authentic South Dakota firefighting memorabilia from the days of Rapid City's first fire brigades – including the original fire pole, ladders, patches, and lots of photographs. Tim is an ex fire officer, and he was in heaven. It was a beautiful conversion and, to cap it off, both the food and the beer were outstanding. We couldn't keep away, eating there at both lunchtime and evenings.

I had never eaten so much in a single day, and I was still hungry throughout. For the record, my food diary for the rest day was as follows:

- Breakfast: 2 yoghurts, large bowl of diced fresh fruit, large bowl of porridge with sugar and raisins and milk, scrambled egg, bacon, 4 pancakes with lashings of maple syrup, loads of fruit juice and coffee
- Lunch: big plate of fish and chips with a mountain of coleslaw, apple crumble and custard, beer
- Dinner: green salad, large plate of pasta with sliced chicken in a rich sauce, creme caramel, beer
- Between meals: about half a kilo of grapes, 2 oranges, 3 bananas

But Rapid City wasn't only about eating. In 1999 a local politician, Don Perdue, had the bright idea of cashing in on the proximity of Mount Rushmore, by commissioning life sized statues of not just four, but all forty-two Presidents of the United States. It took nearly ten years, and involved half a dozen artists who each portrayed the most recognisable characteristics of several presidents. The resulting bronze statues are charming. They are sited at the intersections of the square grid of streets in the centre of town, four at each intersection, facing each other on opposite corners. Some were easy to recognise. President Kennedy (35th President 1961-1963) was right outside our hotel. Others, such as President Martin Van Buren (The Little Magician: 8th President 1837-1841) were new to me. Helping us to sort them all out was an enthusiastic volunteer guide at the excellent little museum. She encouraged us to do the walking tour, right around the town, to visit them all. We were travelling incognito on our day off, not wearing our cycling shirts, so we had to explain that walking wasn't really what we were after. We compromised by visiting a few of the local presidents, either side of lunch, before heading for a lie down, and then more food. Altogether, this was a very relaxed recovery day.

At least, we were relaxed so long as we didn't allow ourselves to acknowledge the direction of the wind that had been strengthening all morning. It reached its peak by mid-afternoon, when the sun was at its hottest. It tore through Main Street, tugging at the presidential statues. We estimated the wind speed at about 30 mph, and it was coming straight from the east. The forecast was the same for the following day, with temperatures well over 100F. And, if the prospect of riding straight into that red-hot gale wasn't bad enough, we were heading out into the Badlands – a very sparsely inhabited region of arid scrubland and semi-desert that has a fearsome reputation to match its name. Gulp....

We left Rapid City, early on the Monday morning, while the air was still cool, and the easterly wind was still only moderate. This was rush hour on Highway 44, heading towards the airport, and the four-lane road was busy in both directions with commuters and with heavy trucks. I was still finding it difficult to adjust to the complete lack of safety barriers on these big, fast, highways. All you get is one strip of tarmac, with four lanes, and two shoulders marked out in white paint. Head on smashes are all too common – we kept seeing white crosses beside the road to prove it. The good news, for us, was that the shoulders were wide. The bad news was that they were strewn with all kinds of debris - glass, animal carcasses, rocks, and bottles.

We need not have worried about the heavy traffic. As on every previous occasion when leaving a town, within ten miles it had all but disappeared; the road was back to two lanes and empty again. Where does it all come from, or go to? Ok, there was the airport, but we hadn't seen a single plane take off or land, so that seems an unlikely entry and exit point. It's mysterious. All this traffic comes from nowhere, and then disappears. It's like the early morning dew – but noisier, and considerably less romantic.

But we had been right to worry about the wind, which was increasing in strength all the time. We rode one behind the other, taking turns to shelter for 5 minutes until the egg timer went off and it was time to take a turn on the front again. There was nothing for it but to try to switch the brain off, and just pedal. My mind began to wander, and I started to hallucinate. I saw a huge diplodocus – a herbivorous dinosaur – in the grassland near the road. Hang on a minute! I wasn't hallucinating. There really was a diplodocus just over there. We stopped and took photos to prove it. There was absolutely no explanation, so we could only assume that it had escaped from the Dinosaur Park back near Rapid City.

After a couple of hours of hard pedalling into the wind, the grassland gave way to sand and scrub vegetation. The heat and the scenery began to feel quite intimidating. There was no chance of a second breakfast today, so our first target was the tiny hamlet of Scenic, with a population of 86, and it was quite a relief to reach it. This was the first habitation we'd seen since leaving the edge of Rapid City some 45 miles back down the road.

Scenic had made the national news, just a few years earlier, because the entire town had been put up for sale. It seems that, over a period of several decades, all the properties had gradually fallen into the hands of a single person, Twila Merill, and she had decided to sell the whole lot, in one go. In July 2011, the 12-acre town and surrounding area - about 46 acres in total - was listed for sale at $799,000. The sale included the post office, Longhorn Saloon, a dance hall, bunkhouse, museum, and two stores. It also included a train depot that is on an abandoned line that was part of the Chicago, Milwaukee, Saint Paul and Pacific Railroad. But you are too late to buy it. A Church based in the Philippines bought the entire town. And, to make the story even more bizarre, the Iglesia Ni Cristo is no ordinary, run-of-the-mill church. It claims to be the one true church - the restoration of the original church founded by Jesus himself - and it teaches that all other Christian churches are apostates. Why the Iglesia Ni Cristo is interested in the town of Scenic remains a complete mystery, since the local paper reports that, since 2011, it has done nothing whatsoever with it.

Our first impression was that we had walked into the set of a spaghetti western. The place was entirely derelict, and seemed deserted. The timbers of the dilapidated buildings were bleached pale grey by the sun, rooflines decorated with animal skulls, the ancient lock up stood empty, its iron cage door swinging in the wind. Tumbleweed blew down the street, and all it needed was Clint Eastwood to make an appearance. But it also had post-apocalyptic overtones, with abandoned and rusting military vehicles, and a group of motorcyclists, including some weird, high powered tricycles, dressed like extras from Mad Max. Perhaps it was the feeling of Armageddon that attracted the Iglesia Ni Cristo.

Anyway, while Tim was messing about pretending to be incarcerated in the lock up, and taking photos (there really was an ancient lock up, swinging door and all, I wasn't exaggerating) I took shelter from the sun on the forecourt of the gas station – the only modern building in town, and the only one that was open. Here, the motorcyclists were a German couple, who had flown over and hired bikes specially for the Sturgis Rally. They were struggling with the intense heat, and they just could not understand how we could cycle in it. To tell the truth, I wasn't very sure myself. It was not yet 11 in the morning, yet it was like a furnace, and we hadn't reached the Badlands yet. Food, and water were needed.

The day's ride was constructed to give a tour of the Badlands National Park and, specifically, to allow us to cycle along South Dakota Highway 240 - the Badlands Loop Road. For 20 miles, this remarkable road runs through a moonscape of strange, wind-eroded rock formations, renowned for their extraordinary coloured layers and known as 'the Wall'. Our route along the Wall ran north west, so the wind would no longer be in our faces (the final time that we would ever cycle a significant westerly section of road), but first we had to keep riding east, to reach the town of Interior, near the park entrance.

After Scenic, we began to see the first bits of Badlands geology - places where the wind had scoured away the sand to reveal small cliffs of sedimentary bedrock. Some of these gave occasional shelter from the wind, but mostly we just battled on one behind the other. Away to the south there were huge vistas across the scrubland, and the noon light had a hard, steely blue edge to it. The roadside fencing began to get bigger and more serious, and warning signs started to appear. It looked as though this might be military land. But no, the warnings said, 'PLAGUE. DANGER. NO ENTRY. RISK OF DEATH.' The unlikely explanation was that the local prairie dogs were infected with genuine, 14th century plague. The plague is caused by the Yersinia Pestis bacterium, usually spread through flea bites, and these flea-ridden prairie dogs were dying of the Black Death in droves, in the 21st century, albeit mostly underground in the middle of nowhere. But, apparently, two people in Colorado had died the previous year, having been bitten by infected prairie dog fleas, and hence the fences. It seemed that we had escaped death by rattlesnake venom in Montana, only to risk the Black Death in South Dakota. The joys of long distance cycling.

After five hours of headwinds we had covered just 75 miles, and reached the town of Interior. I was very tired, but pleased that we had been able to maintain even 15 mph. Interior turned out to be a glorified trailer park, with few fixed homes. The Badlands Park visitor centre, with a posh café, was another few miles up the road but, crucially, it was beyond the turning for the Badlands Loop Road, and the yearned-for relief from the wind. So, we were delighted to find Interior's very basic, community kitchen in a shed beside the road. It was busy with people eating, and we were the only outsiders, so heads turned as we walked in and approached the counter. This was not a place with fancy chalkboards, and there was no clue as to what was on offer.

"Can we see a menu?" I asked.

"It's goulash" was the reply.

"That sounds fantastic. We'll both have goulash".

Delicious and enormous – proper calorie-enhanced cycling food.

At the Park entrance, we had to join the queue with the RVs and motorbikes before we could pay our entrance fee at the toll booths. I'm not used to queueing in traffic on a push bike, but blatant queue jumping couldn't really be justified in these circumstances, so patience was required. Then at last, we reached the Badlands Loop Road, turned left and, hallelujah, we were no longer riding into the wind.

The Badlands are difficult to compare with anything else. They are a three-dimensional maze of gullies, ridges, towers, ravines, rock pinnacles and spikes, up to 200 feet from the bottom of a gully to what was, at one time, the original ground level. These Badlands formations are cut from alluvial and volcanic ash deposits, carved into these fantastic shapes by wind and by water falling in infrequent, but torrential downpours.

Part of the beauty is that each of the layers has a different colour. The 80-million-year-old Pierre shales, the bottom layer of the Badlands geology, are black. They were laid down by a great inland sea and are rich in fossil clams, ammonites, and sea reptiles. Some of this sea mud was then exposed to the air and turned yellow. The next layers are of 35 million years old deposits from rivers and streams. This sand, mud, and gravel, is generally grey in colour. Next come the brown layers of the Brule formation, when the climate supported a savannah, with occasional bright red and orange layers of fossil soils. The youngest, top layers, are layers of ash, of varying colours of grey, some verging towards blue. Volcanic activity, probably originating in the Rocky Mountains to the west, poured vast quantities of wind-borne ash on the plains of South Dakota about 30 million years ago. Soon after this the deposition of sediments stopped, and wind and water went to work to create the eroded landscape that we were cycling through.

The Badlands Loop Road was constructed to show off the most spectacular feature of all - the Wall. This is a continuous face, running for about 20 miles, where the erosion is at its most active. To the north of this cliff face, and above it, all the layers are intact and covered with topsoil and grass. To the south, erosion has worn away the whole lot, leaving scrubland and semi desert, and the ground level is about 200 feet lower. As we started along the road, the dividing line was a simple cliff face. We were at the lower level, with the cliff on our right, and all the coloured layers of sediment were displayed for us to see. But for most of its length, the erosion area of the Wall was far more complex than this, with isolated towers of rock, maze-like gullies, and canyons. The road wound its way through between them. It was spectacular, but for tired cyclists there were some serious disadvantages. Firstly, the road kept climbing from the bottom layer to the top, and then plunging back down again. This gave close-up views of the coloured sediments, from the bottom, and then stunning vistas from 'overlooks' on the top, looking out across the chaotic jumble of Badlands to the south. But it was very tough on the legs. Second, although the canyons were out of the wind, they locked in the heat, with the sun reflecting off the rock walls and the road surface. We didn't have a thermometer, but climbing steeply out of some of these canyon furnaces was by far the hottest thing I have ever done on a bike, the Okanagan Valley notwithstanding. The veins in my temples were hammering out a warning of imminent thermal overload, and I was reduced to a crawl.

Back at the top of the Wall for the umpteenth time, we reached the Conata Basin Overlook. Several RVs were parked up, and people were out, enjoying the view. Now the wind, though still red hot, had a welcome cooling effect on the blood temperature. As things stabilised, and the roaring in my ears subsided, I began to hear the distinctive mewing of an eagle. I looked up, there it was, right above us. There were a pair of them, using the updraft created by the wind hitting the Wall to patrol up and down, hunting for food. These huge birds were a magnificent sight, and ample reason for a longish recovery stop. I got off the bike and walked out into the moonscape of jumbled rock spires, peering down into the multi-coloured gullies all around. I chose an isolated rock eerie and sat atop the pinnacle, watching the eagles soaring overhead. There are some moments of utter peace and contentment that really should last forever, and this was one of them.

For the final few miles, up and down along the Wall,

the eagles were never far away, and I was sad to say goodbye to them as we finally turned north and left the Badlands behind. This final leg was on a dead straight road, on parched grassland, across big, regular undulations. On the crest of each wave, the road ahead was visible against the sky, with rollers disappearing into the distance. With the addition of a large, lollipop-shaped water tower on the final roller, it looked just like Teletubby land. We arrived in the town of Wall, having completed 110 gruelling, but thoroughly enjoyable miles, just as a monster of a thunderstorm broke over our heads. The evening steak had never tasted so good.

Wall's claim to fame is a text book example of how to self-promote not-very-much, and with such stunning success that it has become legendary in the USA, and beyond. Wall Drug started out, in the 1930s, as a local drugstore, just the same as thousands of other small-town drugstores up and down the country. Business was very slow, but then the owners, Ted and Dorothy Hustead, came up with the idea of a mass advertising campaign offering free, ice water to parched travellers heading to the newly opened Mount Rushmore monument. (It's hot round here – have I said?) The highway was plastered with billboards. From that time on, business was brisk. Wall Drug grew into a cowboy-themed shopping mall and department store. Today, Wall Drug includes a western art museum, a chapel, and an 80-foot dinosaur right beside Interstate 90. It still gives away free ice water, along with free bumper stickers with slogans such as 'How many miles to Wall Drug?'. It is said to draw two million visitors a year – a high proportion of the pilgrims to Mount Rushmore. The key to its success was the massive advertising campaign, featuring billboards all along Interstate 90 and beyond. Even though we hadn't been on

Interstate 90, we had seen adverts for Wall Drug all along our route from Billings. It's the American Dream of the little guy who made it big-time. At his funeral, Ted Hustead was described as, 'a guy that figured out that free ice water could turn you into a phenomenal success, in the middle of a semi-arid desert, way out in the middle of someplace.'

So, did we go to claim our ice water, and to see what all the fuss was about? I'm afraid not. We had read the wise words of Bill Bryson, who says: 'It's an awful place - one of the world's worst tourist traps,' (though he sugars the pill in that affable, Bill Bryson way, by saying that he loved it and wouldn't have a word said against it). Besides, we were knackered.

Our motel was the worst yet. It was a utilitarian block of concrete beside the Interstate junction. The room was tiny, the aircon could not keep up with the heat, and the doors and windows didn't fit. When the thunderstorm hit, the water poured in, flooding the sticky carpet. We had to move the bikes from under the window, to protect them. But, after our day's exertions, we slept through most of the storm.

Next morning the talk was of trucks blown over on the Interstate, floods that had closed roads and left motorists stranded, hailstones the size of apples, and a passing tornado. It had been quite a night. Not that we were remotely bothered about any of this. We were interested in just one, critical piece of information. The wind direction.

On top of the hotel opposite was a Star-Spangled Banner, stretched out taut in an already strong wind. It was pointing due east. What a relief! After two days of easterlies, the westerlies were back – and forecast for several more days ahead. The climate records had indicated a four to one ratio of westerlies to easterlies, so it was to be expected, and I had gambled on it in the route planning. But, opening what remained of those tatty, motel room curtains, to see that flag was still one of the best moments of the whole trip. I could not have sustained back-to-back days into a head wind like the previous day's.

Our route out of town took us on to the Interstate for a short distance. The slipway ramp led steeply up onto an elevated embankment, where the wind hit us full in the back, driving us east down the Interstate as though we were motorcyclists, grinning from ear to ear. It may be illegal to cycle the Interstate but, at this speed, they'll never catch us!

The middle of South Dakota is predominantly empty. But we had now reached cultivated land, rather than semi desert. Massive corn fields, already harvested, lined the road. Occasionally there were a few cows, including a belted galloway, and some well-bred horses. The land was very far from flat, and we were cutting across the drainage. But, for once, this didn't bother us. We were being blown up the hills almost as fast as down them.

The road may not have been flat, but it was certainly straight. We spent the day gazing at far off vanishing points that shimmered on a tarmac mirage of water. From across the water, motor cycles, cars, and heavy trucks floated at high speed towards us. Sadly, the road was made of concrete slabs, and the joints were huge, and badly sealed with tar. So instead of floating on a mirage, the reality was the butt-jarring tedium of 'Bu-bump, bu-bump, bu-bump' over all the joints. More than anything else, this rhythm will stay with me as the enduring physical memory of cycling across America.

We reached Midland, after 60 miles, in not much over two and a half hours, and stopped for a mid-morning second breakfast at a gas station diner. Then things changed a little. It seems that, on the prairie you can only have two directions of road; north to south or east to west. It must be in the American constitution somewhere. Anyway, once we left Midland, the road turned the prescribed ninety degrees and headed north. Suddenly we were battling a 30 mph crosswind, from our left, that was threatening to blow us off our bikes, or into the roadside ditch. We rode side by side, taking it in turns to shelter each other, which made a huge difference. Change overs were tricky though, because of the risk of catching a front wheel on a back wheel on the way past. But the main disadvantage of riding side by side was that the roadside shoulder was only wide enough for one cyclist, so one of us had to ride on the left side of the rumble strip, in the road itself. There were very few vehicles, but they were mostly long-distance trucks, steaming through at high speed, with bored drivers playing games on their phones, or whatever they do. Cycling on the road, rather than off on the shoulder, was to sit there, nervously awaiting an appointment with the truck with your name on it. Every time we heard one coming it was a question of making a swift dive back onto the shoulder.

Riding the crosswind was hard enough. To be riding directly into this kind of wind seemed unthinkable, and yet we had somehow managed five hours of it yesterday! As it was, the 22 miles heading north with a crosswind took us an hour and a half.

Eventually, we reached a T junction, the first junction on Highway 14 in 80 miles. This was time to stop, have a drink and a well squashed Danish pasty, and consider which way to turn. Having had so little to think about all day, this was quite a challenge. After careful deliberation, we decided to turn right and head east.

It turned out to be a good choice because, with the wind behind us again, we were soon flying along at around 30 mph or more, at the speed of the wind. We were unable to go any faster, because the bikes didn't have big enough gears. Had we been able to pedal, we'd have been doing 40 mph, easily. We went through 100 miles in 5 hours and 6 minutes, a new record, even with the slower, northerly section, and over 5000 feet of climbing. We reached our destination, Pierre, after 117 miles, in just under 6 hours. As we entered the town, we crossed the Missouri river, now wide and stately. It was two weeks since we had first crossed it, as an infant river, just south of Helena. This felt like a major milestone: next the Mississippi, and then we're almost there. To prove its significance, the Missouri marked the change to Central Time, and 2.30 pm suddenly became 3.30 pm. Time for a lie down.

8 THE GREAT PLAINS

The next day was a bit like Groundhog Day. There was the same wind, the same straight, concrete-slotted road, the same vast, empty cornfields, and just the occasional gas station. Our progress was equally swift and easy. There were some minor differences. There were fewer cattle, some maize, and sunflower fields. The gas stations were more frequent, and always seemed to have a group of local pensioners, chewing the cud in the cafe area. These men, always men, were all very friendly, and interested in our ride. But that was about it. Otherwise everything was much the same as the previous day.

At one point, our hearts sank when we came across a sign saying, 'Roadworks for 35 miles'. They do things on the grand scale in America. Usually this means gravel or wet tar – both pretty disastrous for 35 miles of cycling. But luck was with us. They had just finished the main roadway and were messing about with the verges. They had ripped up all the old, decaying concrete slabs, and the brand-new tarmac was smooth as a billiard table, and had almost no rolling resistance. Soon, we were cruising effortlessly downwind at 30 mph.

Still in the roadworks, we reached a section where only

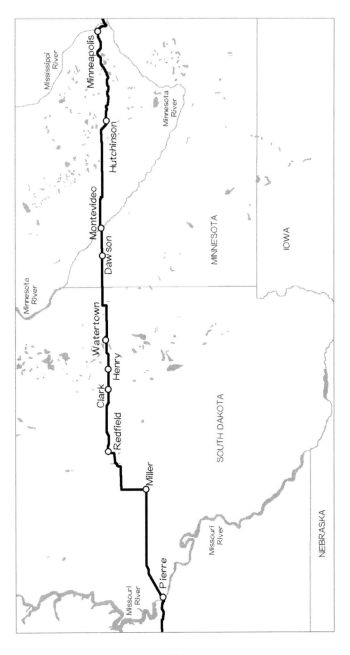

one side of the road was in use. The traffic was being convoyed behind a truck, in alternate directions. But the convoy truck was slow, and soon Tim had crossed between the cones, onto immaculate tarmac in the 'closed' lane. I jumped onto Tim's wheel, and we overtook the entire convoy. The driver of the control vehicle ignored us as we sped past.

At a junction just north of Miller, we reached the end of the roadworks. We stopped at a cafe and, shortly afterwards, a truck driver came in. Lev said he had clocked us doing 35 mph as we overtook him in the convoy, and he was very impressed. He insisted on buying us ice cream. This presented us with a bit of a dilemma, because we were relying on fuelling up with at least 10 times as many calories as an ice cream, but we could hardly ask him to buy us our habitual second breakfast instead. Good manners prevailed. We sat and had ice cream with him, whilst Lev regaled us with his love of South Dakota. He was extremely proud of his home state, and knew it backwards, having travelled around it extensively in his driving job. Clearly, he told us, the Black Hills and the Badlands were the highlights, but he preferred the gentle beauty of the prairie, with its gentle undulations, wide horizons, and dazzling skies. Lev wanted to know the detail of our route through South Dakota, which was easy since, from Wall, it was Highways 14, 45, and 212 – for 350 miles. Oddly, Lev showed no interest whatsoever in our route before or after South Dakota. When I started to provide details, it soon became clear that he didn't know the roads in Minnesota at all, which was a bit embarrassing. At the end of the discussion we didn't have the heart to say, "We're staying on for a proper meal now", so we found ourselves back on the bikes, and short of about 1000 calories each. He was a nice guy though, and the ice cream was good. Thanks Lev.

Groundhog Day continued, as the road turned north again, giving another serious crosswind. More dicing with the traffic as we sheltered each other, side-by-side, one of us in the roadway. The landscape was studded with grain silos - stainless steel cylinders with conical tops. But here they had been destroyed, crushed, and bent as though trodden underfoot by some rampaging giant. Surely this had to be tornado damage. We were right at the northern edge of twister country. In the following few days we were to see several more of these wrecked silos, but no tornados.

At another gas station stop, a young lad of about 13 walked in, fully dressed in wild west style riding gear. His cowboy boots had intricate patterning and spurs, and he wore chaps, shirt, waistcoat, and Stetson hat. We looked outside for the horse, only to see his mum waiting behind the wheel of the family pickup truck. Getting into a pickup truck wearing spurs must be a delicate business. Judging by the fact that we were the only people paying him any attention, non-one else seemed to think this was odd.

But if wearing spurs to travel by car is not deemed to be odd in these parts, it appears that wearing lycra to cycle a bike, definitely is. Even the cattle turned to stare at us as we went past. Later in the day, we overtook a young man driving an old tractor, pulling an acrobat for turning hay. I treasured his look of sheer astonishment, and then his huge grin, as he was overtaken, at speed, by two lycra-clad road cyclists, in the middle of South Dakota.

Even with the northerly, crosswind leg to slow us down, we still smashed yesterday's record for 100 miles, this time clocking 4 hours 47 minutes. Towards the end of the day's ride, approaching Redfield, we came across the first of a series of lakes. Here, at last, after about 200 miles, the road deviated from a straight line, to curve along the lake shore. We turned the handlebars nervously, unsure if we could remember how to do bends. These were beautiful, reed-lined lakes, with isolated houses strung out along the shoreline, each with a jetty and a boat. They were not expensive houses, but they were in a lovely situation, if you fancy living by a big pond in the middle of nowhere.

The lakes themselves have an interesting origin. They are kettle lakes, formed right at the end of the last ice age, about 14,000 years ago. At that time, the glaciers that covered the prairie were melting. Huge blocks of ice floated about in the meltwater, coming to rest as the water drained away, and settling down, deep into the soft boulder clay. These gigantic icebergs, embedded in the ground, took some time to melt, but they filled their own craters with water, and created the kettle lakes. Most of them were still to the east of us, and we were to see many of them over the next few days. Minnesota brands itself as 'The land of 10,000 lakes'.

We had covered our, mostly wind-assisted, 120 miles to Redfield by two-thirty in the afternoon, equalling our 20 mph average speed of the previous day. Only this time, a change of time zone did not shorten our afternoon recovery. After so many day's cycling, this afternoon recovery time had become a ritual - precise and ordered. Check in to the hotel, shower, hand-wash our cycle shirts and shorts in the sink and hang to bake in the sun, upload the day's ride to Strava, put the electronics on charge, lie down to update our blogs and to read, before venturing out for dinner.

In Redfield, dinner was in a converted bank. This was a thriving, family restaurant called Leo's Good Food, that seemed to be pulling people in from surrounding towns. The steak was the best yet, and 16oz went down a treat. From an almost-vegetarian, I seemed to be turning into a voracious, meat-eating machine. Perhaps it was the effect of having only having an ice cream for lunch. But the highlight of Leo's Good Food was the salad bar, not for the salad, but for the location. It was housed in the bank's high security vault, behind a thick steel door with an enormous combination lock. I chose my salad with one eye on the door, worried about being locked in.

The best news of the day came when I looked closely at

the map on the front of my cycle shirt. We had reached the zip, and were officially half way across America.

We left Redfield in completely still, early morning air. After the previous two days of sailing downwind, having to pedal the bikes to make progress came as a bit of a shock. Even by lunchtime the wind was only a gentle, westerly breeze. But I really enjoyed the day, having reached a state of deep contentment with the rhythm of cycling these long distances. I was still loving my new bike, the excellent fit, and the way it just floats along, eating up the miles. In fact, it was beginning to seem as though I was entirely stationary, with the pedalling action making the entire world revolve slowly under my wheels. It was as though I had become my own axis mundi, and it was as close to a transcendental state as I think I have ever come.

I have been asked what I think about all day long, whilst pedalling, and I'm not sure I can give a satisfactory answer. When in the state I was just trying to describe, the answer is, pretty much nothing. At other times, my mind just floats free, thinking about anything and everything. Tim listens to music to while away the miles, but that would spoil it for me. One of the joys of long distance cycling is to let the mind wander off, freewheeling all over the place.

One topic for active daydreaming was that of town names. These were rather disorientating, because the geography of western Europe seems to have been torn up and scattered randomly across the entire area. That morning, we saw signs for Vienna, Naples, Florence, Aberdeen, and Appleby, all in the space of a few miles. Tim has always wanted to see Vienna, and I wanted to see Naples, so when we saw them both signposted down the same turning to the right, we were tempted. But the dirt road leading into the maize fields didn't look very promising, and they were probably 200 miles away.

The countryside was changing subtly. The small towns were becoming closer together and there were occasional copses of wind-stunted trees, the first trees we'd seen since leaving Rapid City. Agriculture dominates everything, mainly cattle and maize. John Deere seems to have a monopoly on the machinery, and some of it is gigantic. A crop sprayer overtook us. Its enormous wheels raised its undercarriage so high off the ground that it needn't have pulled out to overtake. It could have just straddled right over us, and we wouldn't even have had to duck. Decaying agricultural machinery is everywhere, with abandoned tractors left where they refused to start, years ago. Just outside Dawson, there was a graveyard for ancient combine harvesters – a good basis for a museum for some budding entrepreneur. But don't be misled; all the machinery that was in use was high tech and it all looked brand new.

Towns in South Dakota had their population numbers on the sign board. In Clark (pop. 311) there was a talented artist working in scrap metal. In the middle of a grass field, just outside the town, there were nine identical, orange Chevrolet saloons, with white roofs, artfully arranged in two curving lines, as though on the starting grid. Opposite the artist's studio were two giant bicycles, one of which was a penny farthing about 30 feet tall. Tim could not resist trying to climb up to get into the saddle but, unfortunately, the whole edifice lacked a certain amount of structural integrity, and Tim's weight threatened to bring the sculpture crashing down. It was a spectacular leap, as Tim made a rapid exit, just in time.

The town of Henry (pop. 268) had celebrated 125 years, with bunting everywhere and a beautifully painted mural that celebrated The Big Tree, the town's main feature, bang in the middle of Main Street. Closer inspection revealed that the town had been founded in 1882, so the anniversary in question had been in 2007.

This was 2015, so presumably, nothing much had happened in between. Nonetheless, Tim fell in love with the place, mainly because it had the same name as one of his grandchildren, and he set about photographing the lovely, old wooden buildings.

We arrived in Watertown (pop. 21,995) in time for lunch. This was the largest place for many miles around, situated amongst a series of kettle lakes. The lakes were home to a large quantity of wild fowl, including diving birds that I didn't recognise, many types of geese, and heron. But best of all, the lakes had American White Pelican in large numbers. These are big birds, with long, orange bills equipped with a spectacular orange pouch on the underside. As a child, my parents took me to see the pelicans in St James Park in London, and I was enchanted. 'A wonderful bird is the pelican. Its beak can hold more than its belly can'. This was every bit as good.

Watertown also had a memorable coffee house and restaurant called Past Times. It was indeed like stepping back in time and entering a posh English tea room from the 1950s, probably in Harrogate. There was oak panelling everywhere, thick carpets, upholstered chairs, and linen tablecloths. The entire place was full of well dressed women who lunch. What a contrast with our usual redneck gas stations! Once they had recovered from the shock of our entry in full lycra, and everyone had heard about the trip, the ladies who lunch, and the staff, were all very friendly and they served us an excellent chicken salad. We also bought two home-made raisin cookies for later. They were so big that they would have been useful as a replacement, had we broken a wheel.

I had really enjoyed South Dakota but, sometime in the afternoon, we crossed the state boundary. I ate my wheel-sized raisin cookie, and the sugar rush blew me at high speed, about 20 miles into Minnesota. Not surprising then that people round here are generally enormous. One woman was so large in the lower half of her body that she had a horizontal flange where her waist should have been. It was wide enough and flat enough to push a pushchair right round.

If we had been looking forward to different scenery in a new state, then we were to be disappointed. The rolling fields and gentle countryside of Minnesota replaced the rolling fields and gentle countryside of South Dakota. But we were falling in love with the quiet charms of this land, and we were happy enough.

Dawson (pop. 1480) was built around a railroad yard. Enormous silos store the grain before it is loaded onto rail wagons and shipped east. Accommodation had been hard to find around here, and the tiny motel in Dawson, the Picket Fence, was not bookable online. I had had to phone Cindy, the owner, to book and to agree our arrival time, so she knew we were cycling. This explained a phenomenon that only happened once on the trip. On our approach to Dawson, a car pulled alongside and a woman (Cindy, as it turned out) started waving at us, friendly, but slightly manically, before speeding off. We reached Dawson after riding 126 miles in under 7 hours, with very little wind assistance. Cindy was waiting for us on arrival, and wanted to know about the whole trip.

"So where are you heading for tomorrow?" she asked.

"Minneapolis", was the confident answer.

"But that takes 3 hours in the car" said Cindy in disbelief. It was 150 miles away.

"Good luck with that guys!"

We left The Picket Fence early, and cycled into a low, rising sun. The weather had been perfect for cycling since the thunderstorm in Wall, three days earlier - 60F soon after dawn, mid 80s by afternoon, and not a cloud in the sky. There was no wind this early in the day, but after lunch it returned from the west, at about 15 mph. More seriously, there had been no breakfast at the motel, so the first 16 miles were cycled on painfully empty stomachs. Luckily, the miles seemed to go by in a flash. On the outskirts of Montevideo, Tim saw a diner, but I didn't. Nor did I hear him shout, and we cycled right past it, on into town. Frustration ensued, as we cycled up and down the Main Street several times. Reluctantly, we had to accept that there was no café in town, and we cycled back to the diner. This was a very uncharacteristic error. Normally we were razor sharp in working out where to stop, and slick in not wasting time. I had prepared route cards for each day, showing the distances between likely stops and, in the sparsely populated areas, the locations of cafes and gas stations. To add a couple of unnecessary miles to the longest day of the trip was irritating, to say the least.

After breakfast, calm was restored. More long, straight roads, but this time with added entertainment. Flying out of the sun, and diving low over the road, an aircraft screamed over our heads. For a second, I thought we were being strafed. Then it climbed steeply back up, performed a spectacular 180-degree turn, with wings held vertical, before hurtling back down in the opposite direction, straight back over the top of us. It looked for all the world as though this plane was engaged in a dogfight with itself. Was it being flown by a wannabe Spitfire or Hurricane pilot? The huge plume of spray mist gave the game away. This was released from the length of the wings, right over the crops beside the road. This was 'crop dusting', and it became difficult to cycle whilst holding your breath to avoid the spray. Apparently, this is a growth industry in these parts, with new planes being built in large numbers to high tech standards, incorporating GPS guided spray systems. Pilots are well paid, skilful, and in high demand. It wasn't for me though. The show was spectacular, but I felt airsick just watching. And I couldn't help thinking that chucking huge volumes of fertiliser and insecticides around, whilst burning subsidised aviation fuel at an alarming rate, could hardly count as 'sustainable agriculture'. What next? Treat an entire state by using a cruise missile, perhaps?

We had already noticed the money invested in high tech farm machinery, including aircraft. But on the approach to Minneapolis it was the farms themselves that caught the eye. Every farmstead was immaculate. There were large, well-maintained lawns between the road and the crisply painted, usually white, farmhouses, and the timber out buildings were equally well looked after. There was serious money in agriculture around here.

Hutchinson, after 85 miles, marked another distinct transition. The traffic levels on Highway 7 had been starting to increase, and a dual carriageway lay ahead. But whereas, previously, all the side roads had been dirt roads, after Hutchinson there were some tarred alternatives. We stopped in town for yet another chicken salad lunch, and then turned off the main road. For the first time on the ride, we were cycling roads that, in England, would be called country lanes, too narrow for a central white line. These roads were delightful. They had bends in them. They wandered past tranquil lakes, fringed by increasingly expensive houses. They had enough up and down to be interesting, without being hard work. They had hardly any traffic. They were a cycling paradise.

At the tiny town of New Germany, we joined the Dakota Rail Regional Trail. This gave 30 miles of traffic free cycling, on a beautifully smooth asphalt surface, through to the suburb of Wayzata, about ten miles from the centre of Minneapolis. Agriculture here was less intense, with smaller fields. There was plenty of woodland, and paddocks for horses. But, above all, there were lakes. If Minnesota is the land of 10,000 lakes, then I reckon that we saw most of them that afternoon. Goose Lake, Lake Waconia, Mud Lake, Halstead Bay, Langdon Lake, West Arm, Crystal Bay, and the biggest of all, Lake Minnetonka. Many had small beaches, with swimming areas, or marinas.

The cycle track was busy, not only with cyclists, but with roller skaters and with runners. We were travelling fast, so we had to weave our way carefully through the traffic.

We caught up with a huge guy, also travelling fast on a road bike. His enormous calves marked him out as a powerful cyclist, and he reacted to being overtaken by accelerating and drafting behind us. On reading the shirts, he pulled alongside and wanted to chat. When we explained that we had started from Dawson that morning, and were headed for central Minneapolis, he seemed impressed. Anyway, Luke offered to work for us. So, we stuck him on the front, and encouraged him to ride as hard as he could. As Luke's massive frame punched a huge hole in the air, Tim and I sat in line right behind him, getting a fantastic tow. Suddenly we were flying along at 25 mph – not quite what I had been expecting at the end of 150 miles of riding. It was quite an adrenalin rush, because the track was narrow and twisting, and still busy with other people. We hurtled over road crossings, over speed bumps, and wove between road furniture and people walking their dogs. Sheltering tight behind Luke, we couldn't see any of the approaching hazards, so we just had to trust to his local knowledge and good road sense. After several miles of this we were wrung out, both physically and mentally, and we happily said goodbye as he turned for home in Wayzata. Thanks Luke, that was quite a ride!

The lakefront at Wayzata was the perfect place for the final stop of the day. The road was open to the lake on one side, giving great views out across the water to the tree-lined opposite shore, studded with expensive houses. Expensive boats, to match the houses, criss-crossed the lake. The town side of the road was lined with upmarket shops, hotels, and restaurants, most of which had continental-style, outdoor eating areas on the broad sidewalk. We sat contentedly, enjoying the sunshine and the view, and drank the most expensive coca cola of the trip so far. This is the life! It reminded me of the lakes in the Potsdam area of Berlin.

Like so many roads across the USA, the road from Wayzata was sponsored, for litter-picking duties. Sponsors names appear on a board beside the road, every couple of miles. Usually, these were local firms, but sometimes community groups, churches, or even families. We were used to cycling past a mundane rollcall of local businesses. But the well-heeled suburb of Minnetonka provided an eye-catching variation. Here, the Explosive Suicide Punk Rock Band sponsored several miles of road, and a very nice stretch of road it was too. But punk rock just ain't what it used to be. In 21st century America, even subversion has been subverted.

A final few miles of bike track rail line and, suddenly, we could see skyscrapers in the distance, the first since Seattle, 2,400 miles and 25 days ago. We ducked under the freeway, and pulled up in front of a posh hotel, where I had managed to get a remarkably cheap room. For the first time on the trip, we were not allowed to park the bikes at the end of our beds. This was the breaking of a very close attachment, and we were more than a little anxious to leave them locked in a storeroom. Never mind. Beer and steak was needed. We had completed the day's 150 miles in 8 and a half hours, that's an average of 17.5 mph, burning over 9000 calories, and we were very happy with that. More important, we had covered 620 miles in the past 5 days, we were very much on target, and feeling strong. It was time for a day off the bikes.

Breakfast was a noisy affair, and very expensive. Our central hotel was playing host to a national conference of the campaign group, Moms Demand Action for Gun Control in America. Several hundred women of all ages, all wearing red campaign tee shirts, were planning their day's tactics whilst simultaneously laying siege to the breakfast buffet. This was a scary prospect, and for a moment it looked as though there was a danger that we would go hungry. But we managed to inveigle our way into the throng, elbows out, to collect pancakes, bacon, and maple syrup sufficient to replace yesterday's 9000 calories. Sadly, many of these Moms were doing the same, and I don't think they had burned 9000 calories the day before.

But sedentary lifestyles and overeating were not typical of Minneapolis. It seemed quite a different city from any we had seen so far. It had pedestrianised streets in the city centre, and there were proper cycle lanes everywhere, and lots of people on bikes. Parks were busy with joggers. The city was ethnically diverse, unlike any place we'd been since Seattle. There was a large University presence, and the people seemed to be overwhelmingly young, slim, and attractive. In fact, it had quite a European feel to it – a bit like Lyon.

But the most important business for our rest day was getting our bikes serviced. In confident mood, I had booked a service for each bike before we had even left the UK, with the One to One Bicycle Studio and Café, on North Washington Avenue. And somehow, we had arrived, right on time.

This was a fabulous bike shop. It was so laid back that time seemed to stand still. The sense of humour appealed from the moment I saw bike frames on display, hanging from the antlers of the deer heads that adorned the walls. A young lad greeted us, and confirmed that, yes, they were ready to service the bikes that morning. Indeed, he was rather in awe of the fact that Glen, his retired history teacher and ace mechanic was going to do the job. Glen only worked for them part time, in his retirement, but he clearly had quite a reputation. The knocking noise from the front end of Tim's bike had returned over the previous few days, and we couldn't tell whether it was coming from the headset or the front wheel. It took Glen some time, and involved dismantling the headset, but the problem was finally located in the wheel bearing and resolved. It didn't make another sound. Thanks Glen, you are a star. New tyres were fitted, and drive trains lubed and fine-tuned. Meantime, the café served great coffee and cakes, and we enjoyed telling the story of the ride so far.

Glen was slightly puzzled as to why we were passing through Minneapolis at all. The obvious route east from the Black Hills goes south of the Great Lakes, through Indiana and Ohio into Pennsylvania, at least 100 miles south of Minneapolis. But that would have included a huge amount of flat riding on dead straight roads through corn fields. Whilst we had enjoyed our ride across the prairie, five days of it were probably enough. We wanted some variety.

I am not a great fan of urban cycling but, on a long ride, it's good to come in from the wilds every now and again, and to see some city life. But the cities on the route south of the Great Lakes included Chicago or Indianapolis, Cleveland or Pittsburgh, and none of those seemed likely to be very cycle friendly. Besides which, I wanted to visit Niagara Falls and the upper part of New York state. The key to our route was the discovery that there is a ferry across Lake Michigan, about half way up the lake, from Manitowoc to Ludington. The ferry crossing takes about 6 hours, so it would be a rest day. It would keep us off the dead flat plains, enable us to visit Minneapolis, cycle across the states of Wisconsin and Michigan, and then to enter Canada for a couple of days. We would cycle along the north shore of Lake Eyrie to reach Niagara Falls.

So, the next leg of the ride was to take us from Minneapolis, across Wisconsin, to the western shore of Lake Michigan at Manitowoc. The plan was to cover the 365 miles in 3 days. However, the route included a lot of hills, and we were not going to be helped by a prairie tail wind. As we contemplated another big effort, it occurred to me that we could take advantage of the fact that the daily ferry across Lake Michigan did not leave until one o'clock in the afternoon. With a little bit of reworking of the route, we could lose a few miles, and some hills, and cover about 350 miles in 3 days, plus a short morning. The question was, how important was the target of completing 4000 miles in 40 days? We were still on for 4022 miles, but would 40 days and a couple of extra hours be ok?

That evening we visited a British pub. A large group of well-oiled youngsters was playing croquet on the lawn at the rear, and making it sound more like an ice hockey match. I had fish and chips, and a pint of bitter that tasted suspiciously like an American IPA. A committee meeting was held. It didn't take long, and the decision was unanimous. I started rebooking some hotels.

9 THE MISSISSIPPI

Next morning, we decided to avoid the expensive hotel breakfast, with the Moms very noisily Demanding Action for Gun Control in America. The Nicollet Diner, just around the corner, was a real gem. This was a traditional diner, but refitted with spotless stainless steel everywhere, stylish deep blue seating, and crisp, modern lines. The food was terrific too; double stack pancakes, eggs over easy, crispy bacon, and lashings of maple syrup. The clientele was a varied bunch, and the atmosphere very relaxed. In fact, it was so laid back that a dreadlocked, graffiti artist was at work outside, painting a complex design on the wall, not just unchallenged but encouraged. She posed for photographs for us.

Minneapolis is on the Mississippi River, but we hadn't seen the river yet. So, when we tore ourselves away from the diner, we headed straight across town towards the river. The plan was to follow it downstream, for the entire day, first on riverside cycle tracks and then on a 'scenic byway'. Straight away, the riding was slow, as the traffic lights on every intersection switched to red in front of us. This was a new problem. We hadn't even seen a traffic light for days.

The Mississippi passes between the twin cities of Minneapolis and St Paul in a winding gorge, about 100 feet deep. Neither city has much of a waterfront, and the river has quite an industrial feel, albeit recently cleaned up and regenerated. The river was not quite as wide as I had been expecting, perhaps of similar size to the Tyne in Newcastle. Bridges spanned the gorge all along its length. Some, as at Newcastle, crossed at the high level of the lip of the gorge, while others crossed lower down, connecting the roads at river level. There were bridges of all ages, all types of construction, and set at all angles. One of the lower bridges, set at 45 degrees to the river, was the Stone Arch rail bridge, now converted for pedestrians and cyclists, and something of a local icon. We stopped for photos.

Overlooking the Stone Arch Bridge was an enormous flour mill, made up of conjoined cylindrical towers of monolithic concrete, as we had seen back in the town of Concrete, in Washington state. This decaying mill had been converted into a museum, dedicated to the history of the flour industry. Right next door to it was the brand new, ultra-modern, Guthrie Theater; all blue metal cladding and randomly-scattered windows. The theater was, in part, cantilevered out over the West River Parkway, like a bridge with the leg at one end completely missing. This spectacular architecture appeared to defy gravity completely. We cycled underneath with some trepidation. The contrast between the two adjacent buildings could not have been greater, and provided another point of comparison with Newcastle - the Baltic and the Sage.

The river was also punctuated with weirs, at frequent intervals along the gorge. Some of these were old, and had been used to drive machinery in long-defunct mills and factories. Others were modern, hydro-power barrages. Like the bridges, some ran straight across the river, others were angled across. Each one had a large ship lock alongside, to allow the passage of boats. Whilst much of

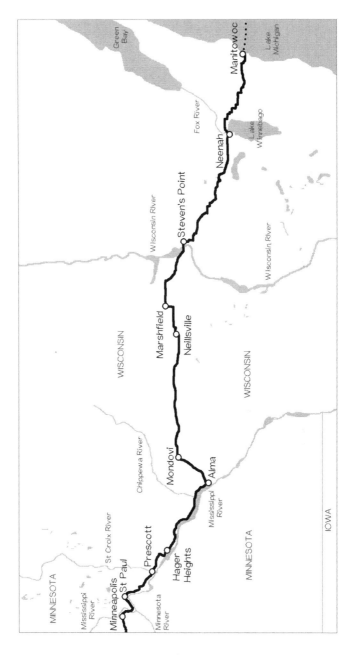

the riverside industry had gone, there were still plenty of barges on the river, and a lot of river traffic.

We spent quite some time at various look-out points, taking in the view, and watching the cyclists and the joggers. But we still had our usual 100 miles to ride, so we had to keep moving. Unfortunately, within a few yards, we came across 'diversion' signs. The riverside cycle route was closed, because a landslip on the cliff above was threatening to take it straight into the river below. We climbed back out of the gorge and threaded our way through the University of Minneapolis campus, trying to follow the diversion signs. This was tricky, because there was a complex network of cycle paths, and multiple directions in which you could be diverted. Normally, this was to be celebrated but, without detailed local knowledge, we didn't recognise any of the destinations on the diversion signs. Strangely, there was no signpost for 'Boston MA'. There was nothing for it but to head southeast on a large road, and hope for the best.

This tactic was successful, but by the time we had regained the riverside cycle route we had only covered about five miles, and it was well over an hour since we'd left the hotel. This was the slowest start to any morning so far. At Ford Parkway, we crossed the Mississippi on a high-level bridge; another significant geographical milestone ticked off. Within another couple of miles, we reached a major confluence with the Minnesota River and, instantly, the Mississippi nearly doubled in size. Perched on the river bluff, protected on two sides in the crook of the rivers, was Fort Snelling.

I found Fort Snelling fascinating, because of the way in which it had played a role in so many of the significant events in US military history, from its founding in 1820 until it was decommissioned in 1946. In the early years of western expansion, it kept the British at bay, and protected the fur traders and the European-American immigrants who were moving westwards. In the Civil War, Minnesota was one of the first states to promise troops to the Union Army of President Lincoln. Nearly 25,000 soldiers passed through Fort Snelling for basic training, first volunteers and then draftees. In 1862, the fort was at the centre of the Dakota War, triggered by resentment at the failure of the US government to pay agreed annuities to the Dakota nation for land ceded. At its conclusion, about 1600 Dakota, mainly women, children, and older people, were taken to Fort Snelling, where they spent three years in a concentration camp, subjected to terrible violence. About 300 people died. Ironically, the site of Fort Snelling, at the confluence of the rivers, was a traditional sacred site for the Dakota nation. During the 1880s the fort was garrisoned by an African American regiment - the 'Buffalo Soldiers' of the Bob Marley lyrics. And, finally, in both the first and second world wars, the fort once again became a processing centre for thousands of recruits from Minnesota. The fort has been recently opened as a museum telling this fascinating story, and restored to look as did in the 1830s. It is well worth a visit.

But none of this was getting us on our way, and the day was slipping away rapidly. Back on the bikes, we followed the cycle path round the bends of the river to reach Minneapolis's twin city of St Paul. An extremely tall and elegant road bridge flew, high across the river. A Mississippi paddle steamer was moored on the far bank, an iconic sight that demanded yet another stop for photographs. But it was still far too early for a second breakfast, so we pushed on.

Downstream from St Paul, progress was still frustratingly slow. Our cycle path ran parallel to a very big, fast, and busy highway, but the cycle path was narrow, uneven, and strewn with glass and assorted rubbish. We were constantly having to give way to traffic joining the highway from side roads, with regular detours to add insult to injury. We began to look, longingly through the substantial crash barriers, at the shiny, smooth tarmac on the highway, both knowing exactly what the other was thinking. No words were exchanged, but a few minutes later we were manhandling the bikes up and over the barriers. Once established on the main road, we finally got the bikes up to a proper cruising speed. It was a bit scary, with trucks passing close by at high speed, but at least we had a small shoulder and were not riding on the main carriageway, and we were making fast progress.

It didn't last long. A few miles down the road we reached a motorway style intersection, where our highway fed directly onto a choice of two Interstates. There was no other route. And, whereas it is merely stupid to cycle the narrow shoulder of a major highway, it is illegal to cycle on an Interstate, and we didn't want an encounter with the law. So, for the second time that morning, we found ourselves climbing the crash barriers and lifting the bikes over the top. But the cycle path had disappeared, and we were in an area of parched wasteland, with grass and scrub bushes up to hip height, hemmed in by fast roads and heavy traffic. Leaving Minneapolis along the banks of the Mississippi was never going to be pretty, what with the oil refineries, rail yards, Interstates, and assorted heavy industry. But being forced to carry the bikes across a rubbish-strewn patch of filthy scrub was getting a bit ridiculous.

This was when I noticed that the state of Zen-like calm that I had been enjoying so much since the start of the trip, was in some danger of vanishing. Ok, I told myself, so we were facing a late arrival at our motel that afternoon, and our attempt to find a faster route had backfired badly. But there was no need to get worked up about it. Time for a break, and some time out.

Jimmy John's Gourmet Sandwich Bar in Cottage Grove turned out to be just the place we needed. It may have looked like a boring, suburban fast-food outlet, but the husband and wife franchisees were lovely people, and the atmosphere was suitably relaxed. Having asked about the ride, as outlined on our shirts, and listened to our morning's tale of woe, they went out of their way to produce the biggest, most calorie-rich breakfast sandwiches you ever did see. Calm was restored.

Things became more straightforward after that. A service road beside Highway 10 led us quickly and safely to the St Croix river, where it joins the Mississippi. Crossing the St Croix, we entered Wisconsin, our seventh state. To our right there was a huge, steel girder railroad bridge, with a central, vertically-lifting section to allow large boats to pass underneath. It was obvious that the lifting was done by cables, left and right at each end, because the twin drums for the gigantic winding gear projected in to the sky, like two pairs of Micky Mouse ears. I would have loved to see it open, but I suspect we may have had to wait a long time.

At Prescott, on the far side of the bridge, we joined Scenic Highway 35, which winds its way south-east along the true left back of the Mississippi. Unfortunately, it wound up and down, as well as from side to side, because the river had cut through a line of rolling hills and the road kept leaving the river bank. This was hard work, and it was red hot again.

At a place called Hager Heights we needed more food and water, but the only place we could see was a drive-thru, fried chicken restaurant. In desperation, we joined the long, slow-moving, queue of cars, mainly pickups. More trucks joined behind us, and people started giving us odd looks, and they weren't friendly. Suddenly, we felt very vulnerable, wearing lycra, astride expensive road bikes, stuck in the middle of a queue of macho drivers in pickup trucks, revving their engines and very anxious to get at their fried chicken. This was just as surreal as cycling through the herds of bison in Yellowstone Park, but there I had felt safer, and less out-of-place. After a few minutes of this standoff, we'd had enough. We abandoned the queue and left them to it. It was several more, weary miles to the next gas station.

But finally, we were in rural surroundings, the road had flattened out, and we were following the bank of the Mississippi. This was more like it. We were looking out over Lake Pepin, which was about two miles wide at this point, formed by a hydro dam at Alma, our day's destination, some thirty miles downriver. The sun sparkled on the water, and a wind had started to blow, right on our backs. I was starting to enjoy myself again. The only slight annoyance was that Highway 35 was very popular with motorcyclists, the first we'd seen since the Sturgis Rally in South Dakota. In small numbers, I have no problem sharing the road with them, but when they start passing in groups of forty or fifty, then it gets very noisy and antisocial. (I feel the same about cyclists, by the way. Small groups are fine, but really large groups can be a nuisance to other road users and café owners alike).

The Hillcrest motel, just north of Alma, boasted the cheapest room of the entire trip, but it was excellent, and had a superb view out over the broadened river. The owners were very friendly, and we ended up in town with them, eating in their favourite bar and restaurant, and being introduced to their friends. True to form, the aspect of the ride that caused the most amazement was the idea that we could travel unsupported for forty days, each with just a small saddle bag. It's not the physical challenge that impressed people, but the idea of living without all the usual stuff. Maybe that's where our high Zen levels came from. Anyway, after dinner, we sat outside the motel, unencumbered by possessions, watching the wildfowl on the river, and enjoying a spectacular sunset.

There was no breakfast to be had in the motel, nor in Alma, so the night before we had stocked up with giant, sticky cinnamon buns, the only thing we could find. It wasn't ideal, but so fuelled we left the Mississippi behind and set off up a side valley, following the Buffalo river. The early morning calm was stunning: there was dew on the grass, deer emerging from the woods, buzzards patrolling overhead. The valley had steep, wooded sides, but the valley floor was flat and about half a mile wide. The river was unmanaged and wandered freely about the natural, uncultivated floodplain. There was willow and alder, and lakes with bulrushes and wildfowl – and all in the mellow, early morning light. Best of all, there was hardly a car to break the spell. This was a beautiful way to start the day, and a lovely 25 miles of cycling, capped off with a huge pancake breakfast in the small town of Mondovi.

After breakfast the landscape changed, with large areas of deciduous woodland interrupted by small fields. Logging trucks appeared on the road, for the first time since the Black Hills, but this time carrying hardwood logs. The tiny hamlets were clearly impoverished, with few facilities and plenty of decaying properties. Near Osseo, we stopped to look at a war veterans' memorial field, with a Cobra attack helicopter stuck, rather incongruously, on a pole. But mostly, the morning just sped by, with Highway 10 purring past under our wheels, helped by a light tail wind.

At Neillsville, we hunted round for a café for lunch. The only option appeared to be Donna's Cozy Kitchen, and first impressions were not good. A dilapidated frontage of peeling paintwork and water-stained brick contained only two, small, high windows so that we couldn't see in. We opened the entrance door with some trepidation. As we had guessed, the tiny interior had also seen better days. Two elderly men were sitting at bare, wooden tables having their lunch, whilst Donna herself presided over affairs from behind the counter. It was clear straight way that our entrance was the most interesting thing to have happened in Donna's Cozy Kitchen for many a long year. But if cosiness is defined by the warmth and generosity of the welcome, then this place lived up to its name. We really enjoyed the chat, and the food. I was starving hungry again, and ate an excellent plate of stew, this not being the kind of place for salad. One of the diners, John, was reassured by the fact that Tim was raising money for cancer research, since that gave the ride a purpose that he could support, and support it he certainly did. First, he presented Tim with a donation, in cash, and then, when we got up to pay Donna for the meal, she smiled and told us that John had already settled our bill. Thanks John, that was really kind.

The third, and final section of the day's ride was different again. We were crossing an area of giant glacial moraines, and the road constantly rolled up and down. The forest thinned out and the trees gave way to fields of maize and grass with well-kept, prosperous looking farms. These had tall, wooden barns in Farrow and Ball paint colours, with Mansard roofs, and one or two tall, concrete silos to store cattle feed. We were in dairy country, but the cows were nowhere to be seen. The only clue was the large number of milk trucks hurtling up and down the highway. Cattle husbandry in Wisconsin works by keeping the herd inside and taking the fodder to them. But in a quietly understated way, rural Wisconsin is very pretty.

The day ended at a large, modern hotel, near the municipal airport on the south side of Marshfield. We had ridden 105 miles in five and a half hours, and were finished soon after 2 pm. It must be admitted that, after seven consecutive days over 100 miles, our interest in afternoon exploring was considerably diminished. So much so that we didn't leave the hotel until 7.30 the next morning. We were very happy to spend the rest of the afternoon recovering, writing our blogs, and reading, and we settled for an evening meal in the hotel restaurant. I am sure that Marshfield town centre has much to offer, but I can't confirm this.

Over the evening meal we worked out that it was exactly a month since we had left Seattle – though it seemed more like a lifetime ago, and a very long way away. In exactly two weeks' time we would be rolling into Boston. The trip was suddenly flying by. Most significantly, we both had the growing conviction that we were going to complete it successfully, though we didn't want to tempt fate by saying too much.

Our arrival at the Marshfield hotel had not gone unnoticed, and the staff spotted the opportunity for some mutual publicity. In the morning, we gave an interview for their very flash website, and posed for photos in our cycle gear. We didn't mind at all, because they had been very helpful, and this was a very comfortable hotel, recently refurbished to a high standard.

Leaving Marshfield, we were soon onto tranquil back roads again. Of all the states we crossed, Wisconsin provided some of the best cycling. The roads were almost car free, away from the few main arteries obviously, and they rolled along gently through some lovely countryside, peppered with lakes and waterways. Wisconsin doesn't have a 'wow' factor – but for relaxed cycling, it is very pleasant. All the previous states we had crossed had relatively few tarred roads, so that we had to share them with the RVs and large trucks. In Wisconsin, many of the minor roads were tarred, all the RVs disappeared, and so did most of the trucks. We could relax more, although most road users across the USA were very courteous and careful.

From Auburndale to Junction City, for about twelve miles, our road ran close beside a railroad called the Soo Line. Soon we heard the familiar sound of a train's horn, catching us slowly from behind. The horn was blowing almost constantly, because of the frequent side roads, each of which crossed the railroad on an unguarded level crossing. The two engines, coupled together, overtook us very slowly. Over the next ten minutes, at least half a mile of industrial rolling stock followed. Then, as the train climbed a long incline, we gained on it, gradually working our way back along the wagons and finally overtaking the two engines. The driver looked up and waved, for all the world as though he was used to being overtaken by long distance cyclists.

Leaving the train behind, we followed along beside the Wisconsin River for a few miles, before crossing it to enter Steven's Point. Here we found an old rail depot that had become a museum. Pride of place was given over to a restored steam locomotive that towered over the depot. We stopped, partly to take photos, and partly because, as usual, we were hungry, and in urgent need of a second breakfast. Three men were working on the locomotive, which was retired from the Soo Line in 1955. They were very keen to tell us about its history, but they soon realised that what we really wanted was directions to the nearest diner. Luckily, this was no problem, and they gave an enthusiastic recommendation to the South Point Restaurant, which was on our route out of town.

We were very grateful to them, because this was one of the best diners we visited. No chalk boards, linen napkins, or table cloths here. This was more like a community centre, packed with at least fifty people of all ages, all of whom seemed to know each other, and all tucking into very cheap and delicious, classic diner food. The room went quiet for a second as we tottered in, unsteadily on the shiny floor, in cleated cycle shoes and lycra. Let's just say that we stood out from the crowd. Once again, people were friendly, once they had recovered from the shock, and had worked out what we were doing. Most important, the breakfast was fantastic, and probably well over 2000 calories.

The rest of the day passed pleasantly enough, following

a series of quiet, country roads. The highlight was probably Chain O'Lakes, a series of beautiful kettle lakes, set in woodland and, as the name suggests, linked together conveniently for canoeing trips. We bought ice cream and watched the boats go past. On the shore of Partridge Lake, outside Fremont, we had an excellent chicken salad at a tiny restaurant that was more like a garden shed. After our meal, we were required to pose, for the second time that day, for photographs, this time for The Porch Restaurant's Facebook page.

The final leg took us into Neenah, on the shore of Lake Winnebago. This had an attractive waterfront park, but it was some distance from our hotel, in the centre of town, and post-ride lethargy set in again. The best feature of the town was its name, which was what my children used to call emergency vehicles when they were little. I amused myself by listening out for nee-nahs in Neenah, and there were plenty.

Our final morning in Wisconsin saw us heading around the north shore of Lake Winnebago and across rolling countryside to the ferry at Manitowoc, on the western shore of Lake Michigan. This was a relatively short cycle ride, but we had to catch the 1 pm ferry, and the addition of a stiff headwind meant that we could not afford to take it too easy. I was glad to roll into town, in time for lunch, knowing that we would have the afternoon off.

Manitowoc is an industrial port, now in decline. During the Second World War, its boat building yards were converted to build submarines and 25 of them saw wartime service. I was very surprised that anyone would build ocean-going submarines so far from the sea, but I guess they were also a long way from attack. Another excellent small museum tells the story.

After lunch, we made our way to the ferry terminal,

where the SS Badger was waiting for us. The SS Badger is a coal-fired steamship, built in 1952 for the Chesapeake and Ohio Railway company to carry its trains across the lake, avoiding Chicago. It is the last working survivor of fourteen that were built to carry railway rolling stock, and the train's passengers, in some comfort. Alongside the SS Badger's mooring at Ludington are the decaying remains of the only other existing steamship, the parts of which are gradually being used up to keep the Badger going. In 1990, when the railway company stopped operating the route, the SS Badger was converted to a car ferry for tourists. But it isn't ideal for the job. It does not have the bow door of a modern car ferry, and it is much narrower, meaning that vehicles can't be turned around, and must be reversed out of the stern door. The public are not trusted to do this, and we sat on the dock and watched as the cars were individually loaded, very slowly and carefully, by members of the crew. We were delighted to see that the railway tracks are still in place on what is now the car deck.

We were very much in holiday mood as we boarded alongside the families of exited holiday makers. We found deckchairs on the sunny side of the boat and amused ourselves by taking photos of our feet, suitably stuck up on the ship's railing. The only disappointment was that the steam engine is not accessible to visitors, because it is tucked away in such a tight space in the bowels of the boat. In fact, from on deck you would never have guessed that it is steam driven. Lake Michigan is notorious for its high winds, rough water, and winter ice floes, but for our crossing it was as calm as the proverbial mill pond. The sun shone as we glided across. Somewhere in the middle we crossed from Wisconsin into Michigan, and jumped forward to Eastern Time, our fourth and final time zone.

I was well aware that the Great Lakes are enormous - the clue is, as they say, in the name. But I hadn't quite realised that Lake Michigan is so big that in the middle you can't see the shore at all, for nearly an hour of sailing. The distance is just over sixty miles, and the crossing takes four hours, which is almost exactly the same speed as we had been cycling. Tim posted the journey on Strava, and it looks quite convincing as a cycle ride, until you notice the blue background on the map! It must be said that sitting on a boat with our feet up was considerably less effort than cycling across, even if it is pan flat. But I am not yet ready to sign up for cruising holidays and after a couple of hours confined to the boat I was bored, even after exploring every available square inch. Luckily, the ship docked in Ludington before I gave way to the urge to fetch my bike for a few laps of the deck.

Well-heeled Ludington, with its marina, expensive shops and genteel restaurants, was a real contrast to post-industrial Manitowoc, with its unpretentious diners. Having lost an hour, it was well past 7 pm by the time we rode into the centre of town and found ourselves a very nice restaurant with an outdoor table, warmed by the evening sunshine. This turned out to be one of the most expensive meals of the trip, but it was well worth it. The setting was lovely, looking along the attractive Main Street of painted clapboard buildings, hung with flower boxes. As we sat there, waiting for our meal, a couple on a reclining tandem stopped, saw our bikes and shirts, and came over to chat. Laurel and Mark, who lived nearby, were very enthusiastic about cycling in Michigan, and had a detailed knowledge of the best local routes. There are low cliffs along this eastern shore of the lake and, according to them, a world-renowned cycle route runs along the top of the best bits. It sounded lovely, and Tim assured them that he would come back and ride it another time. This was partly in response to their obvious disappointment, and even disapproval, when we explained that we were intending to spend precisely two days in Michigan, and that we were planning to speed out of Ludington along the boring main highway, missing all the bits that they loved so much. This wasn't what they wanted to hear.

I understand the delights of savouring the beauty of a specific locality, and of getting to know it intimately. I have my own favourite rides, short and long, at home in North Yorkshire, and I'll always ride them and love them. But this ride was about something different altogether. For Tim and I, covering large distances each day had become an addictive pleasure all of its own. Watching the landscape change as the road sped past under our wheels had become almost mesmeric, and we loved the feeling of well-being that went with it. This was just as well, because our two days across Michigan added up to 260 miles, and we planned to follow those immediately with another 220 miles in two days across part of Ontario, Canada, to reach Niagara Falls. We pulled a map up on a phone to show the route to Laurel and Mike, and it must be admitted that Niagara Falls did look a very long way from Ludington for just four days of cycling. Laurel and Mike clearly thought we were mad, and they were fellow cyclists! Nonetheless, this was a very sociable evening, in good company, and it was dark by the time we finished our steaks, and pedalled off happily to find our motel on the edge of town.

10 THE GREAT LAKES AND NIAGARA FALLS

The forecast was for yet another red-hot day, with wall to wall sunshine, so we made another very early start. Close to Ludington, Highway 10 was busy with commuter traffic but, as usual, after a few miles the traffic thinned out nicely as the road headed due east. This was a pleasant temperature for cycling - the air still held its early morning coolness, and there was plenty of shade from the dense trees of the Huron-Manistee National Forest, through which we were passing. This was always my favourite part of the day. The land was flat, and the road was ruler-straight for the first thirty miles, so we took five-minute egg-timer turns on the front and made rapid progress. There was little in the way of agriculture in these sandy, forested soils, and very few settlements of any kind, not even gas stations. For us, this meant no stops and no second breakfast until the 32-mile mark, when we found Government Lake Lodge, a rustic log cabin, seemingly in the middle of nowhere, beside a picturesque small lake. A patio gave great views of the lake, and the breakfast was first rate.

As we left the Lodge, we realised that right next door was an enormous prison, run by the Michigan Department of Corrections, and surrounded by high security fencing. This was the Lake County Technical Rule Violator (TRV) Center, and it turned out that this forbidding complex houses only the lowest risk prisoners, with the aim of rehabilitating them on release. You certainly don't want to break any Technical Rules in Michigan. Goodness knows what the high security prisons look like. The TRV Center was on the edge of the small town of Baldwin, and along with its associated health and education facilities, it looked as though it was the economic backbone of the town.

Approaching Reed City, we turned off Highway 10. This was not before time, because the highway was getting bigger and busier as we travelled east towards more populated regions. We joined the Pere Marquette Rail Trail, which uses the route of the abandoned railway line from the Ludington Ferry, heading south east towards Detroit. This gave us a fantastic break from the traffic for fully seventy miles, all the way to Midland, our day's destination. It's a shame that they haven't converted the first fifty miles, from Ludington to Reed City, but maybe that's next. The surface was smooth tarmac, albeit with some occasional tree root damage, and the railway gradients were nice and easy. A lot of it was plumb straight for mile after mile. It was quite narrow, and a strip of grass had been cut short, neatly, on either side of the tarmac. Tim said that it looked like a driveway to a grand house that you never arrive at. It was quite disorientating. In front, the path disappeared to a distant vanishing point, and behind, it was exactly the same prospect. Once up to cruising speed, the stroboscopic effect of the ubiquitous lineside trees flashing past meant that it was hard to get a view out to the side, and our sightlines were often restricted to the narrow ribbon of tarmac ahead of us. But at least the rail trail visited a string of small towns, and food was never far away. In one place, the old station

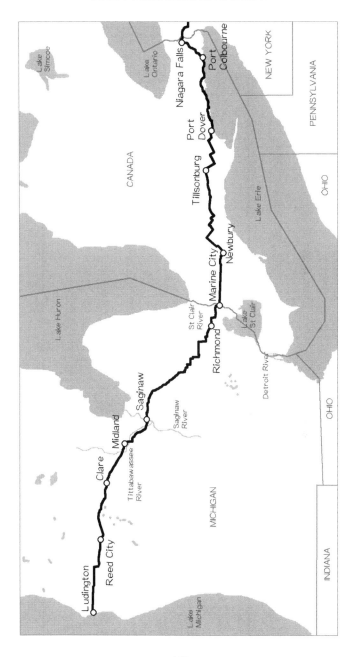

building had been converted to a café. Very convenient.

At Sanford, the rail line met and then followed the wonderfully-named Tittabawassee River. In fact, there was a lot of wetland either side of the line for much of its length, and we enjoyed catching glimpses of wild fowl and herons.

For the first time for a while, the final few miles of the day seemed to take a long time. Perhaps it was the relative monotony of the rail trail, or the effects of an easy day the day before. Whatever the cause, my legs were tired and my body sore, well before we finally rolled into Midland, after 118 miles. But outside our otherwise nondescript hotel on the edge of town was a London Routemaster bus from the 1960s, resplendent in its original livery, albeit advertising the hotel. This was a perfect cue for some mucking about, and soon Tim was lying under the front wheels of the bus with his bike, whilst I photographed the horror crash for his blog. Luckily, there was also a bright red British style phone box at hand for me to summon the emergency services. For a mental health assessment.

Midland was the biggest town we had seen since Minneapolis. It is very much an industrial town, with a huge chemical plant on its outskirts. As we cycled out to the south east the next morning, the plant just seemed to go on and on. It was surrounded by high-security fencing, the like of which I had only previously seen at military installations. There were huge pipes criss-crossing the site, steel chimneys belching fumes, holding tanks of all shapes and sizes. There were access roads for the inevitable tankers and trucks, but also rail lines in all directions. After the peaceful rurality of Wisconsin and north-western Michigan, this was quite a shock.

Once we had crossed back over the Tittabawassee River to cycle the quieter, East River Road, we found ourselves passing the huge, countryside homes of the seriously rich. Enormous front lawns led to detached mansions, well back from the road. Many of these were newly built. Well I guess someone must be making some money out of all this industry. It was just a bit of a surprise to see such places only just out of sight and sound of the chemical plant.

A few miles further on, and things changed dramatically again. Entering the outskirts of Saginaw, our attempts to weave a way through the outlying housing estates on minor roads were thwarted by the state of the road surfaces. It was a bit like entering a war zone. Many of the wooden houses were for sale, boarded up and collapsing, and the concrete road surfaces had turned to crazy paving. There were huge potholes everywhere, and giant lumps of concrete scattered about. Welcome to recession-hit Michigan. After a few minutes of trying to ride at a snail's pace through the chaos and decay, we turned tail and made our way directly to the nearest main road. Only to find that the road surface here was hardly any better. And now we were having to dodge the traffic as well as weave between the potholes.

We travelled north-east through the town, aiming for a small bridge over the Saginaw River – one that wasn't a busy three-lane highway. This turned out to be almost traffic-free, largely because the surface was suspension-wreckingly bad. We tiptoed across at walking pace. But on the other side we entered a different world altogether. Downtown Saginaw was full of smart office buildings, restaurants, and cafes. You would never have known that people were living in some pretty desperate housing conditions, just a few miles away. Bancrofts cafe belonged to the America of chalkboards and sophisticated menus. For hungry cyclists this is a poor alternative to our standard diner fare of pancakes, bacon, and eggs, because the calories are harder to come by, and more expensive. But somehow, we managed to eat sufficient crab cakes, feta flatbreads and cappuccinos, with classical music playing in our ears. Sometimes you must just grin and bear it!

Then it was back out to the suburbs, and the potholes, the 'for sale' signs, and boarded-up houses and shops. It was quite a relief to reach the open countryside, though the road surfaces did not improve at all. The problem is that all the concrete roads – presumably from the 1950s and 60s – are breaking up. Not just gaping joints between the concrete sections – that's a problem right across the USA. 'Bu-bump, bu-bump' over each badly-tarred joint in the concrete was the constant backdrop to the trip. No, here in Michigan, entire concrete slabs have turned to crazy paving, tilted at angles, some four inch thick chunks thrown out on top of the road surface, leaving huge holes. It's a nightmare! It seems that Donald Trump may have a point. Michigan desperately needs infrastructure investment. But the scale is enormous, and it would take a huge amount of money to dig out all the broken concrete and start again. Michigan has a problem.

We were aiming to travel south-east across the inevitable, square grid of roads, with the added frustration of having to bump over the potholes on two sides of every square. The only relief came in the shape of three separate rail trails, each of which was angled helpfully in our direction across the grid, and was beautifully surfaced with new tarmac. Having these on the route made a lot of difference psychologically, even if they did add up to only about 20 miles of our mammoth, 138-mile day. In fact, in our two-day, 260-mile ride across Michigan, nearly 100 miles were spent on these excellent rail trails. Given the state of Michigan's roads, these were a godsend.

During the afternoon we passed through the town of Richmond, and were reminded of Greg and his family, who we had met in Winthrop, in Washington State, right at the start of our ride. It was he who had recommended the third of today's rail trails – the Macomb Orchard Trail

– but, unfortunately, attempts to meet up and ride it together just didn't work out.

This was only the second longest mileage day of the trip but, on bad road surfaces and rolling roads with no helpful tailwind, it was the longest time we spent in the saddle, over eight hours, and it felt like one of the hardest days riding. We were extremely glad to reach the banks of the Saint Clair River, and our motel on the edge of Marine City. This felt like another major milestone, because the Saint Clair River is the border with Canada. It carries the outflow from the vast expanses of Lake Superior, Lake Michigan, and Lake Huron, south into Lake Eire, and hence, via Niagara Falls to Lake Ontario and the Atlantic via the St Lawrence River. For such a significant river, it seemed surprisingly small. Canada was almost within touching distance, at only just over half a mile away. As we sat there, taking pictures, an enormous container ship loomed up from over the distant fields, rounded the bend in the river and steamed right past us, seeming to occupy nearly half of the river's width, and towering over our heads. It turned out to be a very busy waterway, with a constant flow of ships of all shapes and sizes.

We were too tired to face going out again in the evening to search for food, and the motel had no restaurant, so we phoned for a pizza delivery. It's not that morale was particularly low. We had taken a lot of satisfaction from the fact that, at the end of our 30th day of riding, we had covered 3024 miles, which took our average daily mileage to over 100 for the first time on the trip. We were three quarters of the way through, and we felt confident of finishing. But we were properly tired. Still, just two more long days in Canada, following the north shore of Lake Erie, and then we planned to give ourselves a day off the bikes at Niagara Falls. After that, I was very much looking forward to cycling in New England.

It turned out that this first day of cycling in Canada was the only one out of the forty that we really didn't enjoy much at all. The fact that it was the only day without any sunshine may have had something to do with it. But more of that later. Meanwhile, the day started well. The motel in Marine City didn't offer breakfast, so we rode into town, to the Bluewater Ferry terminal, where there was an excellent all-day diner, with a great view from a picture window, straight out over the river. We sat there, enjoying the sight of huge sea-going tankers and container ships passing within yards of our bacon, eggs, and pancakes. It isn't often that big ships sail right past your cafe window while you are having breakfast, so we made the most of it and lingered over extra toast.

There is only one bridge over the Saint Clair River, at its northern end near Sarnia, and it carries Interstate 94 from the USA into Canada. Cyclists are not allowed across and, although I had read reports of the border guards organising lifts to get cyclists across in trucks, this was not something we were going to take a chance on. There is no other road crossing until you reach Detroit, 70 miles to the south, and we were not going there either. So, this meant that the small, and little-known, Bluewater Ferry was very important to us. It explains why I had been so keen to use Greg's local knowledge to check on its continued existence when we had first met him and his family back in Winthrop. The ferry doesn't take trucks, only about 10 cars, and it takes a couple of minutes to cross the river, dodging the big ships. At the Canadian side there was nothing except a jetty and a tiny hut. Border and customs formalities were perfunctory but friendly, and we were welcomed, with a broad smile, to Canada.

The Canadian side of the Saint Clair river was pan flat. There was absolutely nothing in sight except for mile after mile of corn fields and a very occasional farmstead. The roads were called 'lines' - as in the Courtright Line, the Bickford Line and the Oil Springs Line. Ours was the

Bentpath line, which amused us, since it ran due east, ruler-straight for 35 miles. But the amusement was short-lived, since the thickening cloud had brought light rain and drizzle. Worse, an easterly headwind had sprung up and was strengthening all the time. Heads down, we took it in turns to lead into the wind and rain. With very little traffic, and no sign of human habitation for miles at a stretch, this felt as though we had landed on the moon. It was very much what I had been expecting in the Great Plains, but not here. The miles passed very slowly indeed, until we reached the Southside Restaurant in Newbury, for what was more of an early lunch than a second breakfast.

Place names round here had a very Home Counties feel to them. We were in Middlesex County, through which passed the Thames River, but not through Newbury. Strangely, while travelling through Middlesex County we also passed through Shetland and Glencoe. As you can probably tell, there wasn't much else to occupy the mind as we battled slowly on, into the wind.

Crossing the Thames River, we headed south for a while, to avoid London, which really is the largest place around here. We entered the Thames reservation, which is home to the first nation Oneida people. Sadly, for us, the tarmac ran out at this point, and we found ourselves on a dirt road. This was as unexpected as it was unwelcome. I had carefully gone over the entire route, sampling it with Google street view, and following it in satellite view, to make sure that my desire to follow smaller and quieter roads did not lead us astray onto gravel. After a hard day the day before, and then a headwind and rain that morning, the loss of tarmac was badly timed, and I was angry with myself, and afraid that Tim would be annoyed as well. To make matters worse, the gravel was sandy and damp. Our narrow wheels sank into it and became difficult to steer. It clogged in the brakes and coated us in yellow spray. It was foul. But Tim was stoic, as usual.

"Just keep pedaling".

Nonetheless, we were extremely glad to get through the reservation and back onto the black stuff, albeit into the wind again.

The day wasn't the best we'd had and, for the first and only time on the trip, we weren't enjoying our cycling very much. But somewhere to the north of St Thomas, whether on the Talbot Line or the Ron McNeil Line, I can't remember now, we came across something that made us stop and laugh out loud. Parked beside the road was a tanker truck, with a large hose on the roof. It was painted school bus yellow, and on the side, in big letters, was the slogan: 'The Stool Bus', with the strapline 'We'll take crap from anyone'. As Tim said, when we were cycling along for hours on end in heavy drizzle, with little to look at except the intimidatingly straight road ahead, it was great to see some Canadian humour, even if it's only an occasional splash in the pan.

We didn't get much of a welcome when we finally reached Tillsonburg, our destination for the day, after the slowest 106 miles of the trip. The receptionist at the Howard Johnson Hotel on the edge of town, a woman in her 50s, clearly assumed that we were a gay couple, and she made her disapproval obvious. I suspect that other hotel staff had made the same assumption previously, and had been disapproving, but no one else had been anything like so hostile, and we had just ignored it. At this hotel, however, I was quite genuinely expecting a small parcel from Helen, my wife. We had calculated where I would be at the relevant time, and she had posted it out to me, care of the Howard Johnson at Tillsonburg. So, after I had showered and changed, I was able to go back and ask our receptionist, in all innocence, whether the hotel had received a parcel for me, from my wife in England. I have never seen anyone's attitude change so fast in all my life. Suddenly our receptionist was all smiles, she wanted to know all about the ride, and she couldn't do enough to help. Sadly, the parcel had not shown up.

Although the previous day's route had been running parallel with the north shore of Lake Erie, there had been no shoreline road, and we had never seen the lake at all, only mile after mile of corn fields. But today's route looked more interesting. For 60 miles, from Port Dover to Port Colborne, there was an almost continuous shoreline drive. Better still, it curved enticingly around all the small inlets and promontories along the coast, a welcome respite from the dead straight roads we had been riding. And adding to the positive mood that morning was the thought that this day's riding led to Niagara Falls, and a day off the bikes before the final leg of the journey.

But first we had to ride south-east, to reach the shore of Lake Erie at Port Dover. After an enormous hotel breakfast, the early miles were worrying, because the roads were still terribly rough, and a strong easterly wind was starting to blow in our faces. After an hour, even taking our customary five-minute turns on the front, we were struggling to hold a 14 mph average speed. Typically, the wind increased through the day as the heat built up, so we feared that it would get worse, and with 116 miles to ride we were facing another very long, hard day in the saddle.

The first sign of a change in fortune was being overtaken by a tractor, with a pickup truck following in convoy, tight behind it. Now I regard it as a matter of honour, as a cyclist, never to miss an opportunity to save some energy, particularly when there is some free drafting on offer, so I accelerated as first the tractor, and then the pickup came past us, and I dropped in tight behind the pickup. A few seconds later and Tim had closed the gap and joined me. If you have never drafted a vehicle, then you won't know what an enormous difference this makes. Seconds before we had been labouring hard to maintain 14 mph into a headwind and then, suddenly, we were floating along in calm air, effortlessly, at 20 mph. The only snag is, that to make it work properly, you must be in the vortex right behind the vehicle, with your front wheel no more than a few feet from its rear fender. Any further back, and you are in turbulent air that is no help at all. This can go wrong, as Jan Ulrich found out the day before the 2005 Tour de France, when he went through the rear window of his T-Mobile team car when it braked while he was drafting it. This pickup had a rear window behind the driver and, when the guy first realised we were there, he almost jumped out of his skin. Luckily, he didn't hit the brakes. There can't be too many long-distance cyclists in Ontario, so I guess it was probably a first for him – but he relaxed and waved, and the next few miles passed very happily indeed. It's just a shame that the window didn't open so that we could chat. Inevitably, it didn't last as long as we would have liked – tractor and pickup weren't going quite as far as Port Dover, never mind Niagara Falls – but it lifted the spirits.

As we rolled into Port Dover, the sun came out, revealing a very attractive holiday town with cafes, smart shops, and a lovely marina. As usual, our priority was food, so we piled into the nearest diner for a repeat of the enormous breakfast that we had eaten just a couple of hours earlier. Here we got into conversation with Ed, a bearded fisherman. He explained that, before tourism, the port had been home to a major fishing fleet, contesting the right to fish Lake Erie with the Americans. Ed's fishing family had moved here from Hastings, England, in 1910, when the Canadians were recruiting experienced people to staff the fleet. Ed had retired a few years ago, as the fishing industry shrunk. He was very proud of the place and so, with his encouragement, we spent some time wandering around the quay, where small boats were coming in and out of the narrow entrance to the port. The sun sparkled on the water, seabirds flew overhead, and people were promenading up and down eating ice creams. We were reluctant to move on, and yet that was the nature of the journey.

It seems that we were not alone in realising that this is a lovely spot. As we left town, we passed a memorial cross at the spot where, in 1670, two Sulpician missionary priests had claimed the whole of the north shore of Lake Erie for France. They had chosen Port Dover, we read, for its aesthetic appeal and abundant food sources, and the incident was said to be significant in the development of the Canadian nation. I couldn't help wondering whether this approach to land acquisition would work for anyone, and thought of trying to counter-claim it, but we didn't have a suitable flag with us.

If the priests had known that, just over three hundred years later, and a mile from where they planted their flag, the pristine coast would be home to a giant steel works, then they might have thought twice. This plant is dependent on a next-door coal-fired power station for its electricity, despite its relative proximity to the hydro plants at Niagara Falls, and it releases large amounts of mercury into the surrounding environment. Fish and shellfish in Lake Erie have significant mercury contamination. For a steel plant opened as late as 1980, such disastrous environmental pollution on two fronts seems inexplicable. As we cycled the shoreline road, we passed over the huge conveyors bringing iron ore, delivered by ship, from the jetty to the plant. Then a huge belch of steam was released, explosively, from the plant's roofline, making us both jump as though a bomb had gone off. We can only hope that it was intentional, but not aimed at us.

Once we had passed the steelworks, the shoreline road regained its natural beauty. It wandered in and out of small coves, with great views of the emerald blue lake – and the road surface was not too bad either. This section of coastline turned out to be a prime holiday location, but it seemed to be graded, west to east, by social class. First there was very expensive real estate, all Corinthian columns, gated grounds, and expansive lake views. A few miles further east there were more modest, wooden houses, but each with its own small section of beach, and a lake view. A few miles further on, and the buildings were simple wooden cabins and sheds. And finally, as we approached Port Colborne, there were caravan sites and camp grounds. This was a Sunday, and the whole of the coastline was teeming with life. There were people swimming and sunbathing, and the barbeques were out in force. We rode for miles smelling barbecue meat, which was a real torture. The sight of so many people just relaxing, reading, sleeping and sun bathing made us question our own sanity. Had we got this horribly wrong? But, at least, after so many miles of monotonous cornfields, it was good to have something interesting to look at. And even the headwind seemed to have dropped a little.

At Port Colborne we stopped briefly to admire a steel, lifting bridge across the mouth of the Welland Canal. This is the canal, opened in 1829, that links Lake Erie to Lake Ontario, bypassing Niagara Falls. For us, crossing the bridge proved particularly hazardous, because there was no tarmac roadway, just a slippery, open lattice of steelwork, with the mesh spaced just wide enough to trap a bicycle tyre in the slot. Not built with cyclists in mind.

For the final few miles to Niagara Falls, we weaved our way across a grid of small roads, heading towards a strange cloud in the distance. Realisation soon dawned. This was the huge plume of spray from the falls, hanging permanently in the air above, and visible from fifteen miles away. Wow! It also explained why the road signs were warning of freezing fog, though that seemed unlikely in the temperatures we were riding in. Soon we could see the expensive, high-rise hotels, with their iconic views of the falls, and we were back to the clamour and bustle of city life, the first since Minneapolis. Our cheap motel had an iconic view of the main road, and we decided to settle for that and leave the falls for the following day. In the restaurant that evening we were in celebratory mood. Although it seemed quite difficult to believe, we had cycled all the way to Niagara Falls from Seattle. In fact, leaving Seattle felt like a lifetime ago. We had covered 3250 miles in 32 days. The previous four days seemed to have had us flying eastwards, first across Michigan in two days and then across Canada in another two days. Ok, perhaps that should be 'a tiny part of Canada'. Anyway, our 16oz sirloin steaks, and huge slices of American cheesecake were washed down with plenty of celebratory American IPA.

11 FIVE FINGER LAKES AND THE ADIRONDACKS

Visiting Niagara Falls produced a strange mixture of feelings. Standing on the very lip of the Horseshoe Falls, watching the deep, smooth, fast-flowing water just hurtling straight over the edge into space, and feeling the ground trembling with the impact, is very impressive indeed. Unsurprisingly, I had never seen a waterfall on anything like this scale. It was mesmeric. But, in a strange way, it also felt very tame. Pedestrian walkways intruded above, below, and behind the falls, giving safe access to every possible viewpoint. The famous boats, with their colour-coded, plastic-ponchoed tourists, cruised insolently in and out of the maelstrom at the foot. It was hard to believe that, at its heart, there was a natural phenomenon. The canyon and its falls gave the feeling that it might have been designed and built as a giant theme park experience.

Just as I was reaching this conclusion, we found an exhibition about the completion, in 2013, of the Niagara Tunnel Project. This tunnel is twice the diameter of the Channel Tunnel rail tunnels and, at about 6 miles long, it was claimed to be the largest in the world. Carrying water

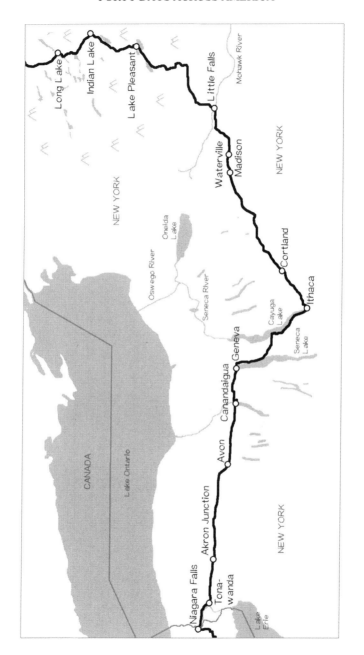

from above the falls right under our motel in Stanley Avenue, it delivers it, at the very high speeds created by the 100 meters vertical drop, to the newly-upgraded, Sir Adam Beck generating station, downstream of the falls. This single tunnel provides enough power to generate 1,600 MW of electricity. This compares very favourably with the largest coal fired power station in the UK, Ratcliffe-on-Soar, which produces about 2,000 MW, but burns over 5 million tons of coal a year.

The exhibition also explained how the flow rate over the falls is tightly controlled by the hydro plants, and that there is an agreed minimum flow rate over the falls in the tourist season. This only added to my sense of the falls as a manufactured theme park. Things are not quite what they seem. In fact, there is a plan to silence the falls altogether for a few months, by building a coffer dam, to repair bridges and parts of the canyon wall. This was last done in 1969, and spectacular pictures of the dried-up falls accompanied the new plans.

After we'd had our fill of superlative facts and figures, we wandered off into the main part of town, which is like Blackpool on speed. There are casinos galore, amusement arcades, fairground attractions, and all kinds of gaudy advertising. We found the newly opened, Niagara Brewing Company, and sampled a very good, English style Best Bitter. We had lunch, and then went back for dinner, in a classic diner with all-you-can-eat pricing. This was good cheap food, but I fear for the longevity of the business if they get regular custom from trans-continental cyclists. We were still packing the food away.

During the afternoon of what would be our final rest day, we began to make some mental readjustments to the idea that we were approaching the end of the ride. We had already noticed more of a tendency to want to linger over interesting places. With a mere 750 miles to ride in the final eight days, what was the hurry? Without doubt, we were beginning to tire of one another's company, as seemed inevitable after nearly six weeks together, and we were looking forward to meeting Helen and Anne, who were flying out to meet us at journey's end. For my part, I wanted to make sure that the trip didn't just fizzle out, and I had planned a route that would allow us to explore some significant parts of New England. The route was to finish with a big loop to the north, right across the Adirondack Mountains, to visit Lake Placid, Lake Champlain and Burlington, in Vermont, before looping back southwards across the Green Mountains, and east to Boston. This was challenging, remote, and hilly country, so it would be a fitting end to the ride. The loop was also designed to be expendable, in an emergency. Had we fallen behind the planned schedule then we could have cut across the neck of the loop and regained up to three days. What I had not foreseen, in non-emergency circumstances such as now existed, was the additional willpower and enthusiasm that would be needed to cycle the whole of the loop, when a more direct route was possible. In the end, we didn't spend long over the decision.

"Are you still up for doing the full 4000 miles?"

"Yes, we may as well, having come this far".

So, we did.

It had rained heavily during the previous evening, and for most of the night. We woke early to drying roads, but low cloud and mist. It felt creepy to be riding through the centre of the normally packed casino and amusement district, just after dawn, when the streets were deserted. We turned onto the Rainbow Bridge over the Niagara Gorge, leading to the frontier post. The view upstream to both falls, American and Horseshoe, was stunning, despite the absence of any rainbow. In fact, there was no colour at all. Everything was in shades of grey, sheathed in mist and spray, with the harsh vertical lines of the high-rise hotels emerging from the gloom.

We had allowed plenty of time for passport control at the American end of the bridge. But, compared to Seattle airport, getting into the USA was very quick and easy. No facial recognition cameras and fingerprinting here, just a quick scan of the passport while a friendly bloke read our shirts and wanted to chat about the ride, and his female colleague quietly admired our legs. No problem.

We set off upstream on a cycle path, right beside the grade six rapids that lead to the brink of the American Falls. The rapids were nearly as impressive as the falls themselves. One huge 'stopper' must have been 20 feet deep. The colossal mass of water was travelling at close to 20 mph, accelerating towards the falls. The bike path ran right along the edge, with no railing at all. The path had seen better days, and tree roots had created sharp ridges across the decaying tarmac. This was not a place to fall off your bike. Or, at least, not to fall off on the right-hand side. Just thinking about it made my stomach tighten, and my head spin. I take back all that I said about the falls seeming tame. When we finally left the bank of the Niagara River, and turned east into Tonawanda, it was with a sense of regret at leaving the Great Lakes behind us. We had thoroughly enjoyed travelling across, and then alongside, Lakes Michigan and Erie and their connecting waterways.

At our breakfast stop in Tonawanda we had "qwaaffy", as pronounced by a waitress from New York, with French cinnamon fruit loaf bread and crispy bacon. Encountering our first New York accent was an encouraging sign of progress. This was another of those working class, community diners, full of single, elderly men, having breakfast and a chat. As ever, we were the centre of attention, and we enjoyed giving a full account of the ride to an attentive audience.

By now, the morning was hot and humid, but drying out nicely. A succession of well-made bike paths allowed us to avoid the morning rush hour traffic in Tonawanda, on the northern fringe of Buffalo. Then a rail trail took us out of town altogether, through the increasingly affluent suburbs of East Amherst and Clarence Centre. Some of these houses were enormous, with huge grounds and swimming pools.

At Akron Junction we joined Highway 5, which we followed, eastwards, for the rest of the day. This had a broad shoulder, a good surface, and light traffic (because our old friend the Interstate 90 runs parallel). The sun began to come through strongly. Best of all, a tail wind began to gather in strength, in response to the sun's heat. This was fantastic, after six days of calm or contrary winds, and terrible road surfaces. After a day's rest, we both felt strong, and it was so good to be back to making fast, easy progress.

Having started early, we had covered 75 miles by lunchtime, when we reached the small town of Avon. Here, we had the biggest Julienne salad of the entire trip. The plates were enormous, and mounded three inches high in the middle with layers of cheese, chicken, and ham. After lunch, we were in danger of arriving at our destination before the earliest check-in time, at 3 pm. To slow things down, we managed to find stomach space for a stop at an ice cream parlour, about an hour later, for the biggest ice cream (but certainly not the best) I have ever eaten.

We ended the day at a lodge just outside of Canandaigua, near the northern tip of the lake of the same name. This was student accommodation, being let to the public during a holiday. It felt very odd to be checking in to a student study bedroom, rather than a hotel room, particularly since my university office is a very similar study bedroom conversion. I tried not to think about work, though, suddenly it was looming on the horizon, with Boston only a week away.

Lake Canandaigua is one of the 'Finger Lakes'. These are series of eleven, narrow lakes, arranged in a north-south alignment like the fingers of two, slightly malformed hands. They were created in a very early period of glaciation, and are so deep that the bottoms are well below sea level. Our plan was to see as much of them as we could, by following the shores of Seneca Lake and then Cayuga Lake, to Ithaca.

The first leg of the day's ride took us to Geneva, properly placed at the head of a lake. The only things missing were the huge fountain, and the views of Mont Blanc. Come to think of it, there was precious little sign of any illicitly hoarded wealth either. There is a State Park at the lakeside, and it had a well-made bike track along the lake shore. Although it wasn't on my pre-planned route, the bike track looked good, and it was heading in the correct direction, so we followed it. This soon proved to be a serious mistake, since it reached a dead end after about two miles, where there was no bridge over the outfall of the lake. It seems that bike tracks around here are not intended for long distance travel, and I remembered, too late, why it wasn't on my route. We refused to cycle all the way back to Geneva and soon spied out a possible short cut to Highway 20, our planned route. It involved climbing a five-foot-high, steel mesh fence and passing the bikes over the top, but we made it. There are so many advantages to having very light weight bikes.

Back on the road, we pedalled south, past well-tended vineyards, the first we had seen. Travelling down the eastern side of Seneca Lake, we soon reached Sampson State Park, which is on the site of a disused, second world war airbase. We accelerated along the former runways, now almost completely covered with green 'matting' from the encroaching woodland, arms outstretched, making suitable aeroplane noises, but failed to leave the ground.

Where is ET when you need him? The park's museum had several vintage aircraft on display outside, and we stopped for photographs.

At the small town of Ovid, we stopped, mid-morning, at a pretty, white-painted, clapboard building that had a restaurant sign outside. It wasn't yet open for lunch, but a very kind woman served us coca cola anyway, and let us sit in the twin rocking chairs on the veranda, between the Stars and Stripes flags. This was a moment of total relaxation. We just needed a pipe and slippers.

Descending to Cayuga Lake, we ran into what was only the third rain we had encountered in thirty-four days of riding. It was just a squally shower really, but it was a spectacular sight, hanging like a dark curtain over the lake as it bore down on us. Several more followed in its wake, and soon it was just like riding in the Lake District. Rain jackets on, or not? Stop and wait for it to pass, or just carry on? We hadn't had so many difficult decisions to make for weeks.

We reached Ithaca, at the southern end of Cayuga Lake, in time for lunch. This is a rich and very trendy town, full of students from Cornell University, just up the hill. We were planning quite a short afternoon's cycling, so we were in no hurry whatsoever. First, we sampled a café for drinks and cakes, before finding a lively lunch spot in the sunshine, but under an awning just in case of further showers. The town was busy, and lunch became quite an extended period of people watching. There was something about the psychology of approaching the end of our ride that was making us want to slow down and savour the moment.

The section immediately after lunch was necessarily slow, since it involved a very steep climb up to the Cornell University campus. We hadn't climbed anything so steep since the Teton Pass, though our full stomachs suffered rather more than our legs. The campus felt very familiar, with original buildings from the 1860s mixed in with high tech, modern blocks, and plenty of current building work. But it reminded me too much of work, so we pushed on, through further rain showers.

Before reaching our day's destination, Cortland, we began to pass triangular warning signs with what appeared to be a carriage drawn on them. Right on cue, we saw a black, covered, horse-drawn buggy coming towards us, with a woman and a child inside. The buggy was open-fronted, allowing the woman to drive the horse, and showing her traditional Amish headscarf and dress. It really was quite a surprise, and a challenge, to see such a countercultural lifestyle apparently alive and well, right in the middle of the USA. We had seen plenty of evidence of the two mainstream cultures in America, and we had cycled through Native American reservations, but here was something radically different from all of them. And this culture was quite widespread, at least locally. Over the next couple of days, we saw several Amish farms and lots more buggies on the roads. I must say that I felt very in tune with their rejection of the internal combustion engine, if not the religion.

Arriving in Cortland took us straight back to one of the mainstream cultures, and not to the privileged one that we had seen in Ithaca. Cortland was very much the poor relation. Here, basic diners replaced the trendy cafes, the shops had seen better days, and the population was noticeably older and poorer. Luckily, our requirements for an overnight stop were quite modest, just a cheap hotel room, and a steak house to eat in, and Cortland was well equipped with those.

When I planned the day's ride from Cortland to Little Falls, it was just a way of getting from the Five Finger lakes to the Adirondack Mountains. On Grand Tours the professionals call them 'transition days'. We weren't expecting much. So, we were delighted when it turned out to be one of those perfect day's riding, when everything comes together beautifully. One of the best of the trip.

The weather was just about perfect. The morning started cool and fresh, with a slight tail wind, and soon there was warm sunshine, with billowing white clouds to give occasional shade for climbing the hills. The road surfaces were consistently perfect, smooth tarmac, and the potholes of Michigan seemed like a distant nightmare. We were picking our way through back roads where there was hardly any traffic at all. The countryside was gently rolling, just enough to provide constantly changing vistas, without ever being too strenuous.

Tim said that it reminded him of the English countryside of the 1960's, before the hedges were removed to make larger fields, and before Dutch elm disease decimated the elm trees. A time when sticklebacks and great crested newts were still common in streams and ponds. I am far too young to remember the 1960s, of course, and I am nowhere near so romantic, but I agreed that this area of New York state was quietly stunning. The rolling hills were heavily wooded in places, a mixture of oak, ash, beech, and elm, with streams and small rivers running through the wooded shallow valleys. Farms were generally rich looking, and not all the farms belonged to Amish people. There was a mix of arable and livestock, mainly cattle, although we also saw a few sheep, which was a first on this trip. I could live here very happily.

At Madison we happened across an enormous antiques fair. There were hundreds, possibly over a thousand, stalls of all shapes and sizes, stretching for well over a mile on both sides of the road, right back into the fields. We had never seen anything on this scale in the UK. There were huge car parks, and people milling everywhere. The road was closed to traffic, so we picked our way through very slowly indeed. I had a near miss with a man weaving across the road, carrying an old chair. Some of the furniture looked beautiful, and I was very taken with an inlaid mahogany dining table, but if bicycles do have any limitations, it is probably in the field of furniture transportation, so I passed.

From the world's biggest antique fair, we moved on to the world's biggest lunch. The options in the town of Waterville were limited and we ended up in a normal looking pizzeria. We each ordered a slice of pizza and a side salad. It turns out that you haven't experienced US portion sizes until you reach New York state. The 'slices' were about a quarter of a large pizza and the chicken 'side salads' contained more poultry than my Christmas dinner. And that's before you consider the huge amount of salad veg and parmesan cheese, and the free garlic bread (nearly a whole loaf). I went in starving hungry after more than three hours of hard work on the bike, having used up about 1500 calories, and I still couldn't quite finish it all. No wonder so many people round here are so obese.

But once the food had settled, we were flying that afternoon. As Tim reflected in his blog, 'whilst wet and windy days may be character building, days like these are pure enjoyment. Pushing hard out of the saddle, feeling the leg muscles burn as you climb the hills. Then putting almost as much effort into to the descent, trying, as usual, to reach that magic 50 mph, legs spinning as fast as possible as you try to catch that downward pressure for extra top speed. It's a feeling of 'being alive' and enjoying the thrill of travelling at high speeds on unknown roads. It's just exhilarating.'

We finished the day with a high-speed descent of a narrow, twisting, canyon, before arriving in the Mohawk valley, and rolling down to Little Falls, tired but happy. The Mohawk valley is a major transport corridor, featuring the Interstate 90, as usual, along with a rail line, the Erie canal, and the Mohawk river itself, winding down to Albany and then south to New York. But it was still surprisingly rural, even with some derelict mills. It reminded me of the Derwent valley, south of Cromford. The town itself was clearly experiencing hard times, with many shops and properties boarded up, or for sale.

Now it was time to tackle the sting in the tail – in the shape of a 200-mile detour to the north to visit the Adirondacks, Lake Placid, and Burlington. I had visited Burlington on a family holiday in Vermont, when our children were small, but Lake Placid had seemed too far to drive from there and we hadn't managed to visit. I'm not sure that the obvious way to remedy this omission was to cycle to Lake Placid, via the whole of America, but that was what I seemed to be doing.

Leaving Little Falls, it required a lot of willpower to turn the bike north, to climb up the steep side of the Mohawk valley and into the Adirondack mountains, when we could have rolled on down the valley towards Albany and reached Boston in three easy days cycling. Having said that, I must admit that my own approach in such circumstances is less clearly virtuous than the application of willpower. I just switch my brain off, think about something else, point the bike in the 'stupid' direction, and refuse to acknowledge that there was ever a choice.

Our morning coffee stop saw us right on the edge of cultivated land, high up on the fringe of the wooded, granite dome of the Adirondacks. This was at the general store in Stratford, a wooden shack, where four old men sat at a table, playing cards, watched over by the elderly owner in a filthy apron. A notice behind the counter spelled out the name 'Obama', with each letter starting the words 'One Big-Ass Mistake America'. I looked round carefully, and then decided that this probably wasn't the time to point out that, by then - towards the end of Obama's second term - it was two.

The Adirondacks turned out to have their own peculiar

charm, and to be quite different from most mountain ranges, in not having linear valleys and ridges. The area is a big granite dome, roughly circular and about 150 miles diameter. The unusual topography is because the granite is too hard to allow deeply incised valleys. Instead, there are isolated, rolling hills, with no ridges. The lower areas have very poor drainage, and there are lakes and bogs everywhere. The average height is only about 1700 feet above sea level, but the landscape is extremely harsh. At another drink stop, we learned that the native Americans never settled here permanently, because the thin acid soils are not fertile, and the winters are much too harsh. The European settlers were the first to try it, and many died. There may be fewer deaths nowadays, but otherwise little has changed. The whole area is still heavily forested, and there are few settlements or roads.

For long distance cyclists, this meant looking at the inside of a lot of ancient forest, with very few long views, whilst the road climbed and fell mercilessly. With no sign of settlements, or agriculture, to break things up, I must admit that this became monotonous after a while. Every corner revealed another, similar, section of wooded road, with another steep climb ahead. Even when the road ran close alongside a lake, you could rarely see it because of all the trees. In retrospect, it was all over very quickly, because there are few strong memories of the day, but it didn't feel like that at the time. It's not that I didn't enjoy it, but the pleasure came from eating up the miles, rather than looking at the scenery. Luckily, we were still feeling strong, and we completed our regulation 100 miles in under six and a half hours, despite over seven thousand feet of ascent.

Our reward was a room in the Adirondack Hotel on Long Lake. This was an old fashioned, wooden building with rocking chairs outside on the veranda, and a lovely view of the float planes moored on the lake. It was a bit like a Victorian, Scottish hunting lodge. Indeed, the hallway contained both a stuffed bear and a stuffed moose, and the wooden walls were covered in trophy heads, mainly deer. Sadly, the room we were offered was dreadful. Two large extractor vents pumped the acrid smell of thick grease from the kitchens through the ancient windows, making it difficult to breathe. Our complaints met a hostile reception, and I was beginning to wonder whether the trophy heads might soon include two cyclists, but, eventually, we were offered a single room as an alternative. Now much as I like Tim, I wasn't sharing a bed with him, and so I volunteered to take the fold-up bed in the corner of the room. Sadly, it turned out to have dodgy springs, but it was too late to complain about that.

At dinner, we noticed that the hotel had another, less charming, idiosyncrasy. The dining room was huge, and it had an ornate, moulded plaster ceiling. But the bedrooms above had been fitted recently with en-suite bathrooms, and the waste piping had been taken straight down though the floor and across the ceiling of the dining room. There were about a dozen rooms, meaning that the beautiful, white feature ceiling was punctuated many times, and criss-crossed by a network of black, plastic pipes. As we sat there, quietly eating our steaks, the silence was punctuated by the sound of flushing, and the gentle gurgle of effluent passing over our heads. Given that we have already established that we were not having a romantic evening together, we saw the funny side of this, and sat there giggling. Though if I owned the hotel, I'd have put the plumber's head on the wall.

12 LAKE CHAMPLAIN AND THE GREEN MOUNTAINS

To add insult to injury, the Adirondack hotel didn't serve breakfast, with or without added drain noises, until eight o'clock. That's no use at all to hungry and impatient cyclists with yet another 100 miles to ride. We left at seven, fuelled on squashed blueberry muffins, left over from the day before. In the end, we were quite glad to get away from what had been the most inhospitable hotel of the whole trip. Which is a shame, since it is such a magnificent old building in a stunning location. We were straight back to the same territory as the day before, soon racking up over 3000 feet of climbing on the rolling, mountain terrain. But now the towns were a little larger, and more frequent, and wealthier. And the lakes and woods were as lovely as ever, albeit under a very grey sky.

We stopped at Tupper Lake after 20 miles. This time we did get a good view of the lake, which was very serene, with acres of beautiful reed beds stretching into the distance. An information board had photographs of the same view in the 1920s, showing that there had been a huge logging industry here. The lake surface was choked with rafted logs, and sawmills lined the banks. It's amazing that there are any trees left. We found the diner in the modern town, and tucked into our delayed breakfast. A four-egg omelette with cheese and ham, loads of bacon, and a double stack of pancakes drenched in maple syrup, washed down with coffee. A ten-dollar bill, received in change, had 'Not to be used for bribing politicians' stamped on it in red ink, apparently part of the 'Stamp Stampede' campaign to get money out of US politics by means of a constitutional amendment.

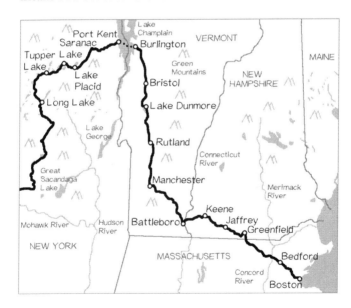

Saranac Lake was another beautiful spot, this time surrounded by expensive homes. The breakfast had proved insufficient to last us until lunchtime, so we stopped to admire the view and to top up on blueberry muffins from a snack shop on the lakefront. That's six blueberry muffins each, by eleven o'clock, which was a new record. The road from Saranac Lake to Lake Placid, was the only section in the Adirondacks with a lot of traffic. As cars, trucks, and pickups whizzed past me I became puzzled. Given that there is basically just one road, with hardly any junctions, how can only one section be extremely busy, and the rest quiet? Do they just drive up and down this same section of road? If so, why? You can tell that the monotony of, by now, about 120 miles of tree-lined, Adirondack roads was finally getting to me.

At Lake Placid, we were finally back to a busy and prosperous, consumer-orientated town, the like of which we hadn't seen since Ithaca. We were also back to liberal America, as evidenced by the quirky, and incredibly messy, café, art gallery and bookshop, run by two gay men. We parked our bikes among the gnomes in the garden, and had a choice of about twelve different salads for lunch. We only just managed to avoid the temptation to have one of each. A fantastic place.

Lake Placid is perhaps best known for hosting the Winter Olympics in 1982. The town itself is built around Mirror Lake, a perfect spot, but now surrounded by shopping malls, and teeming with people. At any equivalent mountain sports venue in the Alps, there would be outdoor sports shops of all kinds, cycle or ski hire outfits, and people intent on doing active things. Here, there was no sign of sporting activity of any kind, and the teeming throng was intent on food, clothes, and souvenir shopping at the enormous malls. We didn't find it very attractive, and soon pushed on.

The route down off the granite dome of the Adirondacks led into a spectacular gorge, formed by the north arm of the Ausable river. We flew down past some big water falls, stopping only briefly for photos. We were heading for Port Kent, a tiny hamlet on the western shore of Lake Champlain, where we were planning to board the hourly ferry across the lake to Burlington, Vermont. With 22 miles to go, I realised that we stood a sporting chance of catching the 14:50 ferry, due to depart in precisely an hour's time, rather than the 15:50. But only if we could maintain 22 mph for the next hour.

It hardly needs saying that Tim was up for an attempt, so we spent the next 54 minutes, as it turned out, team time-trialling furiously down the valley road. Whenever we hit the front we worked flat out, until the egg timer went off. Now team time-trialling is supposed to be about cooperation (taking turns to lead and then to recover), but I am temperamentally unable to avoid an element of friendly competition (trying to match, or even beat, the other guy's effort when on the front). On this occasion, I confess that I became seriously competitive, at least in my mind. Just hanging on behind Tim as he powered, full tilt down the road, was a lung-busting strain, but once back in front, somehow my legs seemed to have recovered enough to go hard again, or perhaps that should be to retaliate. I am not quite sure where it came from, but I released some serious tension during that not-quite-an-hour of high intensity effort. Luckily, Tim was in a calmer frame of mind, and didn't seem to notice.

"Pure pleasure", was Tim's verdict - as indeed it was.

Towards the end of our mad dash, we realised that we were going to make the ferry, and we stopped briefly to look at the Ausable Chasm Falls and to take photos. Then it was downhill, at high speed, to the lakeside and the small ferry, which left promptly, right on time. An odd thing to do, to avoid a short period of forced relaxation by the lake shore, but I am not good at endings, and being so close to the end of the ride had put me in an odd kind of mood.

Our fifth, and final, ferry was a very much smaller affair than the SS Badger. Lake Champlain is very long, north to south, but narrow, and it only took about 40 minutes to cross its width. On board the ferry was a series of photographs showing winter operations. The lake freezes right over, but a single ice-breaker ferry operates throughout the winter, though on the main ferry route, not the one we were on.

I had been looking forward to seeing Burlington, a place I remembered well from a family holiday. It is a large, well-heeled town with a big tourist industry. My original idea had been to find a hotel in town, and to celebrate the fact that we had almost completed the ride, with just three days to go to reach Boston. But hotels in Burlington had proved to be well beyond our budget, and we had booked a room in a cheap motel, some eight miles out of town, near the freeway. But I didn't want to miss out altogether on the bright lights of Burlington, so we stopped for a celebratory beer at one of the chic bars in the city centre. We settled down at a table, outdoors in the pedestrianised street, loud music blaring in our ears, whilst the young college students who were supposedly serving did their level best to ignore the old farts in their ridiculous lycra.

There's something about the psychology of finishing an extended ride that I find very difficult. On the one hand there is a sense of satisfaction, but it is almost entirely cancelled out by the sense of impending losses. The lifestyle had been so carefree and relaxed, and I had felt so well, that I didn't want to give it up. And the whole project had been there, to be looked forward to, for so long that I was unsure what I'd be looking forward to next. Suddenly, the strong IPA began to make me feel melancholy, rather than celebratory. As though to match my mood, it started to rain, and to rain hard. We couldn't be bothered to move indoors, where we would have been even more out of place in our lycra, so we sat there, getting soaked. This wasn't quite what I had had in mind when I had first imagined celebrating in Burlington.

The next morning brought low cloud, but an improving forecast. The plan had been to seek out one of the hardest climbs in the Green Mountains, over the Camel's Hump, to reach the east side of the range. In the planning stages it had looked attractive, and a great way to explore Vermont and the Green Mountains. But a cheap hotel in the correct place for the following night had been hard to find, and we were booked into a motel in Rutland, back on the west side of the mountains, over a second pass. If we got that far, I had reasoned from the safety of my armchair two years earlier, then we'd be so fit that multiple crossings of the Green Mountains wouldn't matter.

But the reality felt different. As I tried to walk to the breakfast room, I discovered that my legs were no longer working. The flat-out time trial the previous afternoon, combined with sitting in the rain drinking beer, and my failure to do any stretching, meant that they seemed to have locked rigid. The prospect of adding over 5000 feet of climbing, over the mountains and back again, when there was a perfectly good, flat, road direct to Rutland, now seemed distinctly unattractive. "Stuff that", we agreed, over yet another meagre motel breakfast.

As it turned out, our new route on Highway 116 was glorious in the early morning mist. Very soon the sun was pushing through and giving glimpses of the wooded, Green Mountain skyline, above and to our left. There was very little traffic, and the loudest noise came from water fowl lifting from the small lakes that still lay beneath the mist. In complete contrast with the Adirondacks, there was nothing wild about Vermont. There were beautiful, rolling, tree-covered hills, sheltering small farms. These were not the immaculate farmhouses with expansive, close cut lawns that we had sometimes seen. Most had peeling paint and rusting trucks in the yard, reflecting a harder existence. There was none of the massive machinery that we had seen out west. Between the farms and the woods there were pretty lakes, with lovingly cared for timber cottages on the shoreline, each with its own tiny jetty. Vermont was a quiet, laid back and unassuming part of the world and, once I had eventually worked the stiffness out of my legs, it was a joy to cycle through it on such a perfect morning.

We had our customary second breakfast in the small town of Bristol, full of interesting, wooden buildings in a variety of styles and paint colours. This was another Sunday morning, and it seemed that most of the town was in the rather smart diner having a late breakfast, presumably just a first one. Our previous Sunday morning's second breakfast in a similar diner in Port Dover, on Lake Erie in Canada, seemed a long way away.

By late morning, the day had developed into the hottest for some time. We made a short, spontaneous, detour to visit Lake Dunmore and Branbury State Park. The lake was a holiday centre, with a beach and water sports, nestling in an idyllic bowl, surrounded by wooded hills. We sat eating ice creams and watching the families playing happily in the water. The only jarring note was an enormous sign, in capital letters, in the window of the general store. 'WARNING SHOPLIFTERS. VERMONT STILL OPERATES CHAIN GANGS'. Maybe Vermont is not quite the liberal state that we thought.

We travelled on south, taking it easy on still-tired legs, and following the gentle valley of the Otter Creek. It was easy to see why they call this New England, and it wasn't just the preponderance of English place names; Bristol, Leicester, Weybridge, Shrewsbury, Sudbury, Wallingford, Castleton, Salisbury. The valley reminded me of that of the river Wylye, north west of Salisbury, England. Except that it was almost too pristine, with no sign of industrialisation and no major highways. Just the untamed river, meandering naturally through small fields and woods, studded with farms that looked as though they were from the 1950s. Perhaps Tolkien's 'The Shire' would be a better comparison. Fanciful, certainly, but 'unspoilt' hardly seemed to do it justice.

Our reverie was interrupted on the outskirts of Rutland, by a 'Road Closed: Diversion' sign. Long experience had taught us that, nine times out of ten, you can get through most road closures on a bike, one way or another, so we pedalled on. But this was the tenth time. It looked as though the bridge over Otter Creek had been swept away in a flood, and the new bridge was in the very early stages of construction. There was just a single pier in the middle of the creek. In similar circumstances, in Germany a few years earlier, I had been allowed to cross a perilous, single plank bridge with just a cable handrail on one side, erected for the workforce, with my bicycle over one shoulder and threatening to unbalance me at any moment. But here, there wasn't even a temporary bridge, so there was no option but to retrace our steps. Annoying, but it was the first time this had happened in the entire ride, and the diversion was relatively short.

That evening, as we sat in the local branch of the 99 Restaurants chain, I recalculated our mileage, and reached an unwelcome conclusion. Because of the decision not to ride up and over the Camel's Hump, we had cut out 15 of our intended miles for the day. Combined with or two earlier minor short cuts, and with just two days of riding left, we were on course to complete a mere 3995 miles – fully five miles short of the target. Having already gone slightly over the 40 days, by adding a couple of hours riding on the morning of what had been planned as a complete rest day on the ferry across Lake Michigan, it now seemed that we weren't even going to complete the 4000 miles. I was annoyed with myself, again. Tim, on the other hand, was blissfully unconcerned.

"You can always ride around Boston for a bit, if you really want to".

Leaving Rutland, the next morning, we cycled south down Highway 7 for about 30 miles to Manchester Center. The previous day's general stiffness and lassitude seemed to have left me and we made rapid progress on another lovely, sunny morning. The approach to Manchester Center was lined with some of the biggest and most expensive houses that we had yet seen, glimpsed over automated security gates and expansive, manicured lawns. So, it was no surprise to find that this small town was very obviously wealthy, with expensive shops and boutiques both small and large. The central shops were small, and housed in traditional wooden buildings with verandas, all painted the same shade of white, whilst the edge of town had newly-built, top-end, 'designer outlets'. The place was busy, and it took two attempts and some advice from a friendly local, to find a café with a free table for our second breakfast. But the only snag with such up-market cafés is that they tend to be very calorie conscious. So, no cyclist friendly monster fry-up here, just a meagre egg muffin.

For the previous few days, everyone reading our shirts had been very congratulatory. After all, we were a long way from Seattle. But no one could quite get their heads round what 100 miles a day means in practice. Whilst enjoying our mid-morning egg muffins in Manchester Centre, the family at the next table asked us when we would get to Boston. The answer, "Tomorrow afternoon", produced confusion, and then consternation, because Boston was still 170 miles away, across the Green Mountains. The conversation dried up awkwardly, with much shaking of heads. They clearly thought we were insane, and probably fantasising, or both.

Undaunted, we set off up the last big climb of the trip, finally crossing the main spine of the Green Mountains, though the climb was small by comparison with those we had done out west. By now it was well over 90F, and we were glad of the shade provided by the extensive tree cover. Normal protocol on big climbs dictates that whoever reaches the top first waits for the other person, before descending. But when I reached the top of the Sylvan Ridge, in second place, there was no sign of Tim. Tim had felt good on the climb, and it was shorter than expected, so he hadn't realised this was the top, already, and he had pressed on, expecting the road to start climbing again shortly. I too was feeling strong again, and our powers of recovery made me regret our decision not to climb the Camel's Hump, the previous day. Perhaps we could have done it, and met the 4000-mile target.

It turned out to be a long way from the summit before we reached anywhere big enough to provide us with lunch. We descended the valley of the not very imaginatively named West River, a lovely, twisting valley with steep wooded sides. As it flattened out towards the bottom, the egg muffins proved woefully inadequate and we were running on empty. I began to hallucinate about food. I think the heat, and the lack of food was getting to Tim as well, because when I caught up with him, in the village of Bond, he was on first name terms with a life-sized, wooden bear he insisted on calling James. It was carved from a tree trunk, and Tim was intent on teaching it to ride a bicycle. We were in a relaxed and happy mood, and it made for some excellent photos.

When we reached Battleboro, the regulation lunchtime chicken salad was long overdue, and very welcome. Immediately after Battleboro, we crossed the Connecticut River and entered New Hampshire, the eleventh of our twelve states. From there to Keene, the destination for our last night on the road, the Franklin Pierce Highway rolled ferociously. The pay-off for all the steep climbing was that, on the descent into Keene, I finally managed to break the 50 mph barrier myself, though not quite beating Tim's record speed into Jackson, Wyoming. On checking in to our hotel, we were delighted to find that a very good friend of mine, another Tim, had managed somehow to work out where we were staying, and had bought us each a congratulatory beer. Thanks Tim!

Apart from drinking Tim's beer, we didn't know quite what to do to mark the final night of our journey. We ended up just going through all our, by now, familiar routines of showering, washing our cycle kit, resting up to write blogs, heading out for a meal, a beer or two, and then back for an early night. I'm not sure if this was due to a lack of imagination, whether it was because we'd grown to like it so much, or whether it was because we were just trying to ignore the fact that the ride was nearly over. In my case, I suspect it was the latter.

It was already hot as we left another brilliant breakfast diner in Keene, at around 7.30 on our final morning. I knew I was going to miss having two breakfasts every morning – eggs, bacon, and a stack of pancakes all covered in maple syrup. Plotting a route into Boston had proved quite difficult, and my efforts to keep us on quiet back roads meant some extra climbing, up forested hills, with curtains of early morning sunlight falling through the trees. The road signs read: 'Moose Crossing'. It was beautiful. Does this really have to stop?

We pulled up at a crossroads in Jaffrey, looking for somewhere for our second breakfast. I wobbled about a bit while trying to look in all directions at once, and we both ended up in the wrong lane, attracting the attention of a police car that pulled across the junction and stopped next to us. As the window wound down, we braced ourselves for a telling-off.

"That's one hell of a ride! Where are you guys from?" was the unexpectedly friendly greeting, as the huge cop behind the wheel read our shirts. We explained the ride, using what was, by now, a well-rehearsed spiel. And then,

"Where do you recommend for a good breakfast?"

Sadly, he didn't come up with some hidden gem, but at least we knew that we hadn't missed anything, as we settled for sandwiches and more blueberry muffins at the gas station. But it was typical of our experience of America to find people who were much more open and friendly than we had any right to expect. And, for the most part, motorists who were tolerant of cyclists and their occasional idiosyncrasies. Tim reckoned that of all the tens of thousands of vehicles that had passed us on the road, only three had let us know that they didn't like cyclists.

We followed Turnpike Road for several miles, until stopped by a 'Road Closed' sign. A group of highway workers were sitting in a van, so we asked whether they thought we would get through the closed section on our bikes.

"No way. The bridge is down. Follow the diversion".

Now in normal circumstances I would have been annoyed at the thought of a detour. So, I think Tim was surprised by my cheery tone as I asked, optimistically,

"How far is the diversion?"

The guy began to explain what sounded like quite a complicated route, through the lanes via another small town. But would it be long enough to add the 5 miles required to get us to the magic 4000?

The diversion was along a very small lane, through woods. But while Tim was scanning the trees, hoping to see a moose, my eyes were glued to my cycle computer, trying to guess how many miles we would add on. Now, I am fully aware that I am stretching your credulity, but I promise you that the detour via Greenfield added five miles. Not only that, but our Garmins rounded each day to the nearest tenth of a mile, and when we added all those together and rounded to the nearest mile, we finished in Boston on exactly 4000 miles. That's what I call efficiency. No energy wasted!

The final day was just one final time through one ritual

after another. A final coca cola stop, a final ice cream parlour for gigantic ice creams and, best of all, a final chicken salad at lunchtime. We must have eaten thirty of these along the way, and this was the best of the lot. There was the usual huge quantity of chicken, but this was top quality meat, not processed slices, on top of a small mountain of crisp, fresh salad vegetables. The waitress at Cliff's Café in Groton looked more than a little bemused as we tried to explain our status as chicken salad aficionados. I'm afraid that our congratulations to the establishment on achieving the Best Chicken Salad in North America Award may not have been received quite as intended. I think she thought we were taking the piss.

After lunch, we crossed the Concord River and reached Bedford, a commuter town on the outskirts of Boston. By this stage, the roads had started to get busier, and quiet byways were harder to find. So, the Minuteman Commuter Bikeway, along a converted rail line, provided a perfect respite from the traffic for about 10 miles into the centre of the city. By this time, we were dawdling along, unable to believe that it was all finishing. If only we had had the foresight to bring champagne and glasses, then we could have toasted each other from the saddle, Tour de France style. As it was, we resorted to taking silly photos. A group of cyclists read our shirts and overtook us with the cheery greeting,

"Not far now, and it's downhill all the way to Boston!"

As indeed it was.

The bike track led us to the north bank of the Charles River and there, across the broad river basin, was the icon skyline of Boston, silhouetted against a dramatically ink-black sky. Suddenly, a flash of lightening crackled between the skyscrapers, followed by a huge clap of thunder. It looked as though the gods had arranged a spectacular reception for us. Our first thought was to press on, to finish before the storm, but the so-called bike path along the Charles River was a nightmare of broken paving slabs and rutted mud and grass. As we crossed the Massachusetts Avenue Bridge to the city centre, the rain had still not arrived, and we sped along a much better bike path on the southern bank. Our luck ran out as we reached the Arthur Fiedler footbridge over the highway on the approach to Boston Common. The storm broke spectacularly over our heads, with torrential rain, punctuated by thunder and lightning. I was in a strange mood, not enjoying the tension of being in limbo, so close to the end and yet not quite there, and it wasn't clear whether the storm was reflecting my emotions or adding to them. Anyway, I was all for ignoring the deluge and just pressing on, but Tim was, very sensibly, having none of it. Instead, he found a shelter underneath the concrete bridge. We stood there for what seemed like hours, but could only have been a few minutes, stuck with a stream of tourists, families with buggies and shopping bags. I wasn't in the mood to chat.

Eventually, I couldn't wait any longer, and I pressed on, with Tim following reluctantly, into what was, by that time, merely steady rain. Then it was round Boston Common, through Chinatown, across the Summer Street bridge over Boston Harbor, where the rain finally stopped, past the Tea Party Museum, and on out to Pleasure Bay. This was as far west as we could go. We had run out of continent. We stopped at the back of the beach, leaned our bikes against the seawall, and looked at each other in disbelief. We had done it – right on schedule. Exactly 4000 miles, right across the USA in 40 days, give or take a couple of extra hours, pretty much exactly as planned all that time ago.

Pleasure Bay had seen better times, and was deserted. People were obviously getting their pleasure elsewhere these days. There was absolutely no one there to witness our achievement, or to take our photos. And in some ways, I was glad about that, because it had been a very personal goal that I had set myself. My first assumption was that I would have to do the whole ride on my own, but I hadn't been sure about committing to that. With hindsight I could see that there is no way that I could have achieved it, nor enjoyed it in the way that I had, if Tim had not been willing to bring his friendship, resolution, and dependability to the enterprise. In the absence of an audience, we pottered about rather aimlessly, taking souvenir photos of each other, and the bikes. Being English, we even shook hands. They say that it's the journey, not the destination that matters, and in our case, it's just as well.

On reflection, we had seen a wonderful, varied continent, and had nothing but kindness from people along the way. Here are some assorted statistics:

- 40 days of riding (plus a couple of hours)
- 253 hours in the saddle
- 4000 miles (Waterfront Park, Seattle to Pleasure Bay, Boston)
- 15.8 mph average speed
- 147,000 feet of ascent and descent (5.5 Everests, in old money)
- 5 punctures
- 32 chicken salads each (approx.)
- 35 hot and sunny days
- 3 hours of rain
- 3 or 4 days of headwinds
- 12 days with strong tailwinds that arrived just when it really counted, on the big mileage days across the Great Plains.

We couldn't have hoped for better. The bikes behaved impeccably throughout, coping with everything thrown at them, and proving completely reliable. My Bianchi Infinito CV fitted me like a glove, was ridiculously comfortable for a fast road bike, and I felt that I could have floated along on it forever, had the Atlantic Ocean not intervened.

But since it had, and with our choice of directions seriously curtailed, we took a final glance at the scene of our triumph, and turned back westwards, towards our final hotel. But first, there was one last job to do, and that was to remove the pedals from our bikes, ready for packing for the flight home. We were not carrying a heavy pedal spanner all the way, just for that, but even this detail had been carefully planned in advance. The idea was to borrow one from a bike shop that I had found, just around the corner from our hotel. I secretly thought that this might have the added bonus of getting us the adulation that had been so singularly lacking at Pleasure Bay.

With high hopes, we pushed our bikes into the Cambridge Bicycle Shop. It was full of cool-looking dudes at least half our age, and very busy. The bearded guy behind the till hardly looked up. Once he realised that we weren't going to buy anything, and that we wanted a favour, he was even less interested. No one even glanced at our cycle shirts. Suddenly, we were far too proud, and too reserved, to ask,

"Do you know where we've cycled from?"

We removed our pedals quietly and left, slightly deflated. We hobbled and limped the final few hundred yards to our hotel, on foot, pushing our pedal-less bikes, hamstrung by our cleated cycle shoes and stiff legs that had long ago forgotten how to walk. Passers-by stared at us pityingly, no doubt wondering what disaster had befallen us.

They say that one of the many things that the English like to boast about, is not boasting about their achievements. By this standard, I should say that the conclusion to our journey, anonymous, shambling, and unheralded, was a triumph, although a little more dignity would have been nice.

ABOUT THE AUTHOR

Andy Hill is a retired university lecturer who is fanatical about cycling. With Helen, his wife, Andy has enjoyed many long distance cycle touring holidays, all over Europe. You can find his cycling blog at: www.urebank.eu